# ARMOURED WARFARE
# IN THE
# BATTLE OF THE BULGE
# 1944-1945

# IMAGES OF WAR

# ARMOURED WARFARE IN THE BATTLE OF THE BULGE 1944-1945

## Anthony Tucker-Jones

Pen & Sword
**MILITARY**

First published in Great Britain in 2018 by
**PEN & SWORD MILITARY**
An imprint of
Pen & Sword Books Ltd
47 Church Street
Barnsley
South Yorkshire
S70 2AS

ISBN 978-1-52670-175-6

*Frontispiece*: An SS-Panzergrenadier runs past burning American equipment, heralding the Battle of the Bulge.

Typeset by Concept, Huddersfield, West Yorkshire HD4 5JL.
Printed and bound in England by CPI Group (UK) Ltd, Croydon CR0 4YY.

Pen & Sword Books Limited incorporates the imprints of Atlas, Archaeology, Aviation, Discovery, Family History, Fiction, History, Maritime, Military, Military Classics, Politics, Select, Transport, True Crime, Air World, Frontline Publishing, Leo Cooper, Remember When, Seaforth Publishing, The Praetorian Press, Wharncliffe Local History, Wharncliffe Transport, Wharncliffe True Crime and White Owl.

For a complete list of Pen & Sword titles please contact
PEN & SWORD BOOKS LIMITED
47 Church Street, Barnsley, South Yorkshire S70 2AS, England
E-mail: enquiries@pen-and-sword.co.uk
Website: www.pen-and-sword.co.uk

# Contents

# Introduction

Early in the morning of 16 December 1944 German artillery shattered the silence of the fog-shrouded hills of the Ardennes region of Belgium and Luxembourg. Behind the barrage waited twenty-five German divisions, ten of which were armoured. Their task was to smash their way through the weak American defences on a front extending from Monschau in the north to Echternach in the south. Adolf Hitler hoped to repeat his remarkable victories of 1940 when he had thrust through exactly the same area. His target was Antwerp.

Hitler knew that the British and American forces were overstretched and that the relations between the Allies were often strained. In addition, the Allied strategy since the Normandy breakout had showed little flair and the German forces, although driven from Antwerp, had ensured the Allies could not use the port until the end of November 1944. In the meantime the Allied advance could best be described as plodding.

Aside from the scale of Hitler's surprise attack, the other shock for the Allies was the appalling weather. Whereas the Wehrmacht and the Red Army had fought through three winters on the Eastern Front, apart from in Italy this was the first winter endured by the British and Americans on continental Europe. While the Germans had some idea what to expect, the American forces were often woefully prepared for the bitterly cold weather. The poor conditions also greatly curtailed operations by the Allied air forces, which had enjoyed air superiority throughout the summer of 1944.

The Battle of the Bulge, as it became known, was characterised by heavy snow that swathed the ground, impeding progress on both sides. The photos of the battle show just how bad the conditions became. Just four days after the German attack commenced the temperature plummeted and snow set in, making the battlefield more reminiscent of Stalingrad than the Western Front. The Ardennes proved to be no winter wonderland but a place of savagery and sudden death. Although the Germans were better prepared than their opponents, they too were to suffer from the extreme cold. Freezing fog covered the winter landscape, hampering visibility and making it difficult to distinguish friend from foe.

Under such conditions the scattered farms, villages and towns gained even more tactical significance. While good fields of fire were important, so were shelter and warmth. Being caught out in the open overnight made it very difficult for men to fight effectively the following day. However, more often than not the troops of both sides had to endure the freezing temperatures with little more than a shallow foxhole or local woods for shelter. Lighting a fire was almost impossible as the flames and smoke soon attracted unwanted attention from snipers, artillery and mortars. Uniforms and boots became wet from sweat and froze, lowering the owner's body temperature even more.

The ground became so hard that the easiest way to create foxholes was by using explosives. After the fighting was over the US grave registration units faced the gruesome task of retrieving thousands of frozen bodies. To add to the woes of the combatants, the tanks and other vehicles, even when whitewashed and covered in snow, gave away their positions thanks to their tell-tale tracks of churned-up snow and mud. This attracted enemy artillery fire and fighter-bombers.

The Battle of the Bulge in the winter of 1944 was a result of the extraordinary recovery of Hitler's panzer and infantry divisions following a series of defeats on both the Eastern and Western Fronts. The battle was immortalised by the inaccurate 1965 movie of the same name and the vastly superior award-winning *Band of Brothers* television series that appeared in 2001. The latter took great care to make the fighting look as authentic as possible.

By the end of 1944 common sense and strategic necessity dictated that Hitler would hold back his rejuvenated formations for the defence of the Rhine and the Oder – these were the great natural barriers that protected the Nazi heartland. Both the Eastern and Western Fronts had all but collapsed and Hitler needed to husband his reserves. The onset of winter convinced the Allies that they could settle down to attritional warfare that would see the level of combat greatly reduce.

Instead, Hitler launched a daring offensive, hoping that his panzers' charge through the Schnee Eifel would unhinge the American and British push on the Rhine and prolong the war. Although American forces in the region were weak, often inexperienced and in some cases battle-weary, it was a tall order because the panzers had to get across the Our, Amblève, Ourthe and Meuse rivers, secure the Losheim Gap and take Trois Ponts and Stoumont on the Amblève as well as the vital road junctions at St Vith and Bastogne. The whole operation was a desperate race against time and the panzers simply could not afford any hold-ups.

Nonetheless Hitler convinced himself that if he could recapture the port of Antwerp, this would deliver a serious blow to the Allied war effort. While the Allies were recovering from this setback, he could then turn east and carry out a similar operation against the Soviet advance in Hungary. With hindsight, the likelihood of Hitler's Ardennes offensive succeeding was very slim. The crippling lack of fuel and reserves, plus the paucity of air cover by the Luftwaffe, meant that as soon as the clouds lifted Hitler's attack was inevitably going to lose momentum.

However, at the time the battle was touch and go, especially for the men on the ground. The Allies were caught completely off guard and it was German mistakes that helped save the day for them. For a while the bad weather grounded the Allied air forces and many American units were either overrun or surrounded. Some inexperienced units performed very poorly, while others showed grit and determination – this was most notable at Bastogne and St Vith. Although the latter fell, the successful defence of the former greatly hampered the German attack by tying up the panzers.

Once General George Patton had marshalled his tanks and cut his way through to the battered garrison at Bastogne, the writing was on the wall for Hitler's offensive. Tantalisingly, the 2nd Panzer Division managed to fight its way to Celles just east of Dinant on the Meuse. By then, though, the weather had lifted and Allied fighter-bombers pounded anything that moved. Out of fuel and ammunition, Hitler's forces had little option but to give up their hard-won gains. After six weeks of fighting the Americans were back where they had started at the beginning of the battle. Foolishly, Hitler had exhausted the last of his offensive power in the West. At the same time, Stalin's winter offensive forced Hitler to turn his attention back to the Eastern Front.

The Battle of the Bulge became one of the most photographed battlefields of the Second World War as both sides' troops were accompanied by film crews. In particular, the Germans provided some of the most iconic and enduring images, with their film of triumphant Tiger II tanks rumbling past captured GIs. Another image that became a staple of subsequent books on the battle showed German paratroops hitching a ride on a Tiger II through snow-covered forests. Ironically, though, the Tiger IIs failed to deliver the results hoped for and were greatly restricted by the unforgiving Ardennes terrain.

Indeed, what made the battle so memorable was the bitter winter weather. Only in the mountains of Italy and Tunisia had the Allies encountered such conditions before. The Red Army, having already fought through three Russian winters, was well acclimatised, but for the British and Americans the snows came as a shock. Summoning the strength to fight in the snow despite being cold and hungry was no easy feat. The Germans for their part marred what was a highly audacious operation by committing a series of repugnant war crimes against both the American GIs and Belgian civilians. Not only did they leave a swathe of death and destruction across the Bulge, but also a trail of wanton murder.

## Photograph Sources

All photographs in this book are sourced via the author. Many of the better known photos of the Battle of the Bulge have been included not only for the sake of completeness but also because of the outstanding quality of the shots. By this stage of the war both sides knew how to take a good photo and shoot exciting newsreel footage for propaganda purposes. Many of the stills are in fact prints taken from newsreels.

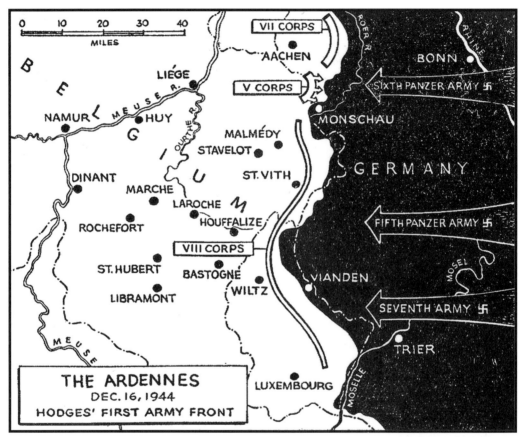

American and German positions at the start of the Battle of the Bulge. To stand any chance of capturing Antwerp Hitler's panzers had to cross the Meuse at Dinant, Namur or Liege.

# Chapter One

# Hitler's Miracle

Field Marshal Bernard Montgomery's attempt to seize a crossing over the Rhine at Arnhem in the Netherlands had ended in embarrassment. Although American airborne troops had successfully secured the bridges at Eindhoven and Nijmegen, the British paras were thwarted by the quick-thinking Waffen-SS at Arnhem. This had forced Montgomery to shift the emphasis of his operations to the west and the Scheldt estuary in an effort to clear the approaches to the vital port of Antwerp. As the weather deteriorated, it soon became apparent that General Dwight Eisenhower, the Allied Supreme Commander, was going to lose his wager with Montgomery that the war would end by Christmas.

The Allies advance began to get slower and slower. Between late September and mid-December 1944 the Allied position along the entire front was broadly the same. To the north Monty's 21st Army Group, with the British on the right and the Canadians on the left, had bogged down on the River Maas, with a small salient just to the south of Arnhem. Further to the south was General Omar Bradley's US 12th Army Group, which was struggling towards the Roer and Aachen. In particular, the battle for the Hürtgen Forest had cost the Americans 33,000 casualties in the space of two months. The need to take the Roer dams before the Germans blew them up had contributed to Major General Troy Middleton's VIII Corps being spread so thinly in the Ardennes sector.

Only to the very far south had any real progress been made, with Lieutenant General George Patton's US 3rd Army advancing through Metz and to the Saar river. This acted to protect the flank of the US 6th Army Group that had reached the Rhine at Strasbourg after fighting its way up through southern France. Even this success, though, was threatened by the stubborn German Colmar Pocket. Eisenhower's broad front strategy had essentially resulted in a dangerously weakened Allied centre since the end of the summer.

Despite all Germany's setbacks, General Alfred Jodl, Chief of the German Operations Staff, had begun planning for a major counteroffensive in the west. On 6 September 1944 at a meeting at OKW (Armed Forces High Command) head-quarters in Rastenburg Hitler had identified three problems facing such an operation:

secrecy, supplies and Allied air power. The first was to be ensured by instigating a vigorous need-to-know policy; for the second, Germany's weapons industries under the very capable Armaments Minister Albert Speer would have to step up production and the offensive forces would be prioritised; but the issue of the Allied air forces could only be tackled by launching an attack under the cover of bad weather. In order to meet all these criteria it was concluded that 1 November 1944 would be the earliest a counterblow could be struck.

Over the next few weeks Hitler and Jodl examined their maps showing the Allied advance. It was obvious that Eisenhower's broad front was soaking up all his resources to the extent that he lacked a strategic reserve that could counter any German breakthrough. This meant that the squabbling Allies would be very slow to react to an assault as they sought to redeploy forces from elsewhere. Hitler and Jodl's eyes kept coming back to the region where the Allied centre was plainly poorly defended.

By 20 September 1944 Hitler had convinced himself that the Ardennes region was the answer to all his problems on the Western Front. The almost mountainous Eifel region was very heavily wooded, which made it ideal for concealing his gathering forces. Five days later an energised Hitler outlined his vision to Jodl's staff. He argued that a substantial breakthrough would ensure that the panzers could get across the Meuse river between Liège and Namur, followed by an advance to Antwerp that would split the Allies. He explained how the panzers would attack in the centre while the infantry protected their flanks to the north at Monschau and to the south at Echternach.

The main blow would come from his two rejuvenated panzer armies, consisting of both armoured and infantry divisions. The plan was that a preliminary artillery bombardment would be followed by the infantry advancing across a 50-mile front who would seize all the Americans' forward positions. This would then open the way for the panzers to strike. The latter, adopting 1940 Blitzkrieg tactics, would bypass any enemy pockets of resistance, leaving them to be mopped up by the infantry. The tanks were to cross the Meuse on the second day, hooking north-eastwards around Brussels and on towards the coast before the Allies realised what was happening.

It was at this point that Hitler's aspirations became a little hazy, clearly clouded by wishful thinking. Getting to Antwerp was ambitious enough, but on top of this he seems to have assumed that the Anglo-American alliance would collapse into chaos. Whilst there certainly were ongoing military and political tensions between the two leading Allies, having got this far since D-Day it seems fanciful to imagine they would simply give up, even if they received a major military shock. In part Hitler was desperate to stall the Allies so that he could concentrate his forces on the Eastern

Front. Since late June 1944 Joseph Stalin's Red Army had made enormous gains following its destruction of Hitler's Army Group Centre.

In Hitler's mind he wanted to emulate the Prussian hero Frederick the Great, who in 1762 had miraculously snatched victory from the jaws of defeat. The problem was that Hitler alone was the driving force behind his Ardennes offensive; he set the agenda, not his experienced generals. Had they been involved in the planning they would doubtless have pointed out that attacking along a narrow corridor without air superiority was a recipe for disaster. On the occasions when his generals were allowed freedom of manoeuvre, they could achieve quite remarkable victories, but this required a great degree of flexibility and thinking on your feet.

Hitler's victories in 1939–1941 had been partly due to his armed forces being able to respond to a fluid battlefield. The conditions in which the Ardennes offensive was to be conducted were simply too restrictive. The weather and the wooded hills were not conducive to the rapid advance of his armoured and mechanised divisions. Nor were there sufficient reserves to handle any major problems in the path of the attack or on the flanks. Hitler's generals should have warned him that if the Americans clung to the major road junctions and communication centres then the attack's timetable would inevitably come off the rails. But Hitler would not listen to any objections, branding them defeatist; instead he carried the day with his overriding conviction they would succeed.

In the meantime, while the German planners struggled to solve their problems, there was also the issue of massing sufficient forces. As was increasingly the case by this stage of the war, Hitler looked to his elite Waffen-SS to blaze a path for the army. In late September 1944 Field Marshal Gerd von Rundstedt, Commander-in-Chief West, was instructed to recall both I and II SS Panzer Corps so they could be refitted. Whilst they did need re-equipping, they were also to secretly form the core of a newly created SS Panzer Army. Under the command of the highly experienced SS Oberstgruppenführer Josef 'Sepp' Dietrich, the 6th SS Panzer Army was to form the key strike force on the German right. It was responsible for the attack between Monschau and St Vith.

This formation's infantry units, along with the bulk of those assigned to the other participating armies, were to be provided by the newly raised Volksgrenadier divisions. These were built around a cadre of infantry divisions destroyed in Normandy or on the Eastern Front. Although fleshed out with new recruits, they also included army veterans returned from hospital as well as large numbers of Luftwaffe and Navy personnel. The plan was that ten of these divisions would be ready by 20 November, with a further three available by the end of the month. The intention was that a total of twenty Volksgrenadier divisions could be in the field by 10 December 1944. They would bolster the existing infantry divisions already defending the Ardennes sector with the 7th Army in the south and the 15th Army to the north.

The second armoured assault force was to be General Hasso von Manteuffel's 5th Panzer Army. This was to cut its way through American lines between St Vith and Wiltz. It was withdrawn from the front line in late October for refitting. All four armies were to come under Field Marshal Walther Model's Army Group B. Technically Model was responsible to Rundstedt, but in reality he answered to Hitler at OKW. The whole operation was codenamed *Wacht am Rhein* ('Watch on the Rhine') – which implied that it was of a defensive nature. It was also dubbed Operation *Herbstnebel* ('Autumn Mist').

On 21 October 1944 Hitler briefed his special forces' thug, SS Obersturmbann-führer Otto Skorzeny, about the supporting operation known as *Greif* ('Griffon'). Skorzeny was to infiltrate American lines using the so-called 150th Panzer Brigade. This was recruited from English-speaking German troops who were to pretend to be Americans using US uniforms and vehicles. Once behind enemy lines they were to create as much chaos as possible to impede American movements and assist the German advance. The brigade was also to capture at least two bridges over the Meuse.

The following day Hitler laid his plans before Generals Siegfried Westphal and Hans Krebs, the Chiefs of Staff to Rundstedt and Model respectively. Both men came to the same conclusion: that this was a rushed job and the objectives were too broad. In response to their concerns, their superiors were quick to offer critiques to Hitler. Both Rundstedt and Model understood perfectly well what was achievable and what was not. Both were sceptical about Hitler's notions of a war-winning grand slam.

Rundstedt argued that they should set their sights on fighting their way to the Meuse with the intention of trapping those American forces facing the Siegfried Line. This would help ease some of the pressure on their defences during the winter. Model also proposed that they should scale back their plans, with the 5th Panzer Army striking in the Ardennes and the 15th Army from Aachen with the intention of trapping as many American divisions as possible. Predictably, Hitler was not receptive to the idea of smaller operations.

Hitler's only concession was to delete the 15th Army's role in *Wacht am Rhein*. In fact, he had little choice as Allied attacks at Aachen and the Hürtgen Forest made it impossible for the 15th Army to redeploy its divisions. The start date for the offensive also slipped first to 10 December and then to 16 December. In Hitler's favour was the poor condition of American defences in the region. They consisted of exhausted veterans and green troops who had only just come into the line. To make matters worse for the Americans, thanks to German deception operations they had been lulled into a false sense of security.

On 11 December 1944 the final orders for the Ardennes attack were issued and three days later the attacking units moved up to the jump-off points in the Eifel region. Altogether, Dietrich could muster about 450 panzers and assault guns. From north to south he had four panzer divisions (1st SS, 2nd SS, 9th SS and 12th SS), the 3rd Parachute Division fighting as infantry, and four of the new Volksgrenadier divisions (12th, 246th, 277th and 326th).

On Dietrich's left was Manteuffel, also with four panzer divisions (2nd, 9th, Panzer Lehr and 116th), plus the 15th Panzergrenadier Division, but as none of these was at full strength he only had 350 armoured vehicles. These armoured units were supported by four Volksgrenadier divisions (18th, 26th, 62nd and 560th). To the south General Erich Brandenberger's 7th Army had no tanks and could provide only five divisions (79th Infantry, 212th, 276th and 352nd Volksgrenadier, plus the 5th Parachute).

OKW had practically no reserves to speak of. These were comprised solely of two full-strength divisions (3rd Panzergrenadier and 9th Volksgrenadier) and two elite brigades (Führer Begleit and Führer Grenadier). These could only be deployed with Hitler's authorisation. Nonetheless, despite their shortcomings, Hitler's total forces amounted to 275,000 men, 1,900 artillery guns and 950 armoured fighting vehicles. At such a late stage in the war this was a simply miraculous achievement.

Field Marshal von Rundstedt, CinC West, inspecting German defences. In late 1944 Adolf Hitler wanted to launch Operation Watch on the Rhine or Autumn Mist to capture Antwerp. Rundstedt cautioned they would be better limiting the operation to trapping American forces against the Meuse river but Hitler would not heed such caution.

(**Opposite, above**) Following the failure of Field Marshal Montgomery's attempt to get over the Rhine at Arnhem, General Dwight D. Eisenhower, the Allied Supreme Commander, seen here flanked by Generals Bradley, Gerow and Collins, adopted a broad-front strategy to defeat Nazi Germany.

(**Opposite, below**) American GIs supported by an M5 light tank plod past a decapitated Panther. After their victories in Normandy and Lorraine, the Allies' supply lines became overextended, resulting in their generals constantly vying for resources.

(**Above**) Monty photographed in the summer of 1944 with Generals Bradley and Patton. He would spectacularly fall out with his American colleagues over the Battle of the Bulge.

(**Opposite, above**) Men of the US 1st Infantry Division, which formed part of General Hodges' US 1st Army, on patrol in Belgian woods. By the autumn of 1944 the Ardennes region in Belgium and Luxembourg was poorly defended, presenting Hitler with a tempting target for an attack.

(**Opposite, below**) For Watch on the Rhine Hitler could muster only about 150 Tiger Is (seen here) and Tiger IIs. He also planned to use the heavy Ferdinand and Jagdtiger tank destroyers but few were available.

(**Above**) Panzer IVs on the way to their units. During the autumn of 1944 Hitler set about re-equipping his panzer divisions to create two panzer armies. The factories of Armaments Minister Albert Speer pulled out all the stops.

Panzer V Panthers being unloaded from their flat cars still in their factory finish. Wrecked Panthers would become a favourite subject for Allied photographers in the Ardennes.

SS-General Josef 'Sepp' Dietrich was placed in command of the newly created 6th SS Panzer Army. Its job was to attack between Monschau and St Vith.

Massed Panther tanks. For his Ardennes offensive Hitler secretly gathered a powerful force of almost a thousand tanks and other fighting vehicles.

Hummel self-propelled guns of the 1st SS Panzer Division being shipped to the front. At the time of Watch on the Rhine the 1st SS was short of Hummels. Along with the 2nd SS, 9th SS and 12th SS this division formed part of Dietrich's panzer army.

A German Fallschirmjäger mortar crew in action in the Hürtgen Forest, the scene of bitter fighting through the autumn and winter of 1944. Two German parachute divisions were to be involved in Hitler's Ardennes offensive.

The Hürtgen Hotel – a farmhouse used as headquarters by a unit of the US 8th Infantry Division. Some units who had fought in the Hürtgen region were sent to the Ardennes to recuperate as it was considered a quiet sector.

Hitler created twenty Volksgrenadier divisions from mauled infantry and Luftwaffe field divisions, fleshing them out with young recruits from the Kriegsmarine, such as this sailor, and the Luftwaffe. Two such units that employed naval personnel were the 18th and 352nd Volksgrenadier Divisions.

A British tank crew enjoying a cigarette and a mug of tea. General Horrocks' XXX Corps would be called on to help stop the Germans at Celles.

An M16 Multiple Gun Motor Carriage keeping an eye on a local forest. The Allies wrongly expected that the wooded Ardennes would be quiet over the winter.

# Chapter Two

# 6th SS Panzer Army Strikes

Sitting in the path of Hitler's armoured steamroller in the winter of 1944 were just six American divisions numbering about 75,000 men. These units, through no real fault of their own, were in somewhat of a muddle. To the north, facing Dietrich's right, were two divisions from Major General Leonard Gerow's V Corps, the 2nd and 99th. The latter had only been in the line for about a month and was disrupted by the 2nd moving through its positions to advance towards the Roer Dams. In addition, the movement of the 2nd Infantry Division had created a weakening to the south extending for 2 miles in the region of the vital Losheim Gap. It was this gap that Dietrich had earmarked for his advance.

This area was defended by an element of the 2nd Division, the 14th Cavalry Group, but it was poorly deployed and stretched thinly to compensate for the absence of the rest of the division. Confusingly, the 14th Cavalry Group was still under the command of Middleton's VIII Corps, which inevitably was likely to cause problems if the unit was called upon to support Gerow's troops.

The most northerly of Middleton's units was General Alan Jones' 106th Infantry Division. This had only just arrived at the front and had been directed into the German Schnee Eifel region to take the place of the 2nd Division. This area was German-populated and consisted of a salient made up of steep valleys and small sleepy villages. The 106th was exposed, and Manteuffel's right flank was tasked with chopping off the salient.

To Jones's south was Major General Norman 'Dutch' Cota's veteran 28th Infantry Division. This had been sent to the Ardennes to recover from the mauling it had suffered in the Hürtgen Forest. Cota's men had to hold a 23-mile front facing the Our river over which Manteuffel's armour would pour. On Cota's right were elements of another inexperienced division, the 9th Armored, which was later to claim fame by grabbing the bridge at Remagen over the Rhine. A single combat command was occupying 6 miles of front, while the other two commands were held back as Middleton's mobile reserve. They would have to fight off General Brandenberger's troops from his German 7th Army. Also in the firing line was the veteran 4th Infantry Division, which was likewise recuperating after Hürtgen.

On 16 December 1944 the German preliminary bombardment lasted about 45 minutes. The gunners had not really been given the chance to target effectively because of the need for complete secrecy in the Ardennes. As well as Skorzeny's 150th Panzer Brigade commando force, cutting a path for the 1st SS and 12th SS Panzer Divisions were Kampfgruppe Peiper and Kampfgruppe Kühlmann respectively, each formed from their division's panzer and panzergrenadier regiments. They were to lead the way up the roads to Trois Ponts, Stavelot, Malmédy and Elsenborn and on to the Meuse south of Liége at Amay and Huy. Support was provided by half a dozen other kampfgruppen.

While the Americans on the receiving end of things were able to ride out the storm, the shelling did cause some confusion and severed communications. Many units were cut off from their chain of command so had no real idea of what was going on or what was expected of them. This meant that the opening day was soon to become a series of small unit actions that would cost the Germans crucial time.

In the north Dietrich had first to barge the US 99th Infantry Division out of the way to take the Elsenborn Ridge, before breaking through the Losheim Gap. On his right this task fell to the 3rd Panzergrenadier, 12th and 277th Volksgrenadier Divisions with the 3rd Parachute Division on his left opposite Losheim. After the opening barrage the German infantry and sappers advanced under the cover of fog into the American lines.

This sounded like quite a formidable force but this was far from the truth. General Walter Denkert's 3rd Panzergrenadiers were 20 per cent under strength and lacked 40 per cent of their equipment. The division had suffered heavy losses during the fighting around Metz and later Aachen. Its armour consisted of a single tank battalion. Both the Volksgrenadier divisions were fairly weak and lacked veterans. The 3rd Parachute Division under General Wadehn had to be rebuilt after Normandy using rear echelon Luftwaffe ground personnel. It officers and men were largely inexperienced.

Dietrich had a small supporting airborne operation codenamed *Stösser* ('Falcon'), under Colonel Friedrich August von der Heydte. This was to involve a parachute landing a few miles to the north of Malmédy in the Baraque Michel mountain region behind the US 9th and 2nd Divisions. The German paratroops were to grab the Baraque Michel road junction and hold it ready for the 12th SS Panzer Division's swing northwestwards towards Liège. A second drop was to be conducted south of Eupen and the Meuse. At 0400 von der Heydte found himself kicking his heels at Lippspringe airfield still waiting for half his men who were unable to join him due to transport problems. This forced him to postpone his mission.

Von der Heydte's command numbered just over a thousand men, but as German paratroops tended to be used as infantry few had even made a practice jump. All the parachute regiments had been ordered to supply their best men for this special operation, but inevitably von der Heydte ended up with the dregs that no one wanted. To make matters worse, he was having to go with his arm in a splint, as he had injured it a few weeks earlier in an aircraft accident in Italy.

As a daylight drop might alert the Allies, the landing was to have been made in the dark, just a few hours before the ground offensive commenced. Von der Heydte pointed out to Dietrich that dropping his inexperienced parachutists into the local forests and onto the moors at night was suicidal. Dietrich reassured him that he would only have to wait a few hours before his panzers arrived at the road junction. In this case it was to be a unit of 70-ton Jagdtigers, which were hardly very mobile.

Meanwhile, on the ground Dietrich soon found that the men of the US 99th Infantry were not going to be a pushover. The defenders at Buchholz station beat off their attackers; likewise at Rocherath and Krinkelt the Americans did not withdraw, and they also held out in the far north in the Monschau-Höfen area. However, things did not all go the Americans' way. At the road junction at Lanzerath a platoon of infantry was overrun by the 3rd Parachute Division. At Manderfeld a squadron of the 14th Cavalry Group was forced to withdraw south while the rest of the unit was destroyed, thereby opening up the Losheim Gap.

For the 3rd Parachute Division its success had been hard won and Dietrich was forced to commit the 12th SS Panzer Division sooner than he wanted. The snow on the roads and the lack of bridging to get over the Our resulted in a huge sprawling traffic jam. It was clear that Dietrich's headlong dash through the American positions to the Meuse was rapidly bogging down.

It was not until just before midnight that day that Colonel von der Heydte's parachute operation finally took place. Some 112 Junker 52 transport aircraft took off from airfields near Paderborn. The drop was not a success; on the approach the transports came under fire and the inexperienced parachutists were scattered from the Rhine to the Hautes Fagnes. Some even ended up beyond Aachen in the US 9th Army's area. Another group of 200 men came down near Bonn, miles behind their own lines. In total three-quarters of von der Heydte's force were dropped inside German lines.

The unfortunate von der Heydte was briefly knocked unconscious when he landed. Upon coming round, he found just 20 of his 1,200 parachutists. Three hours later he had managed to round up 150 of his men, but it was evident they were not strong enough to hold the Baraque Michel road junction against American counter-attacks, especially if they involved tanks. Colonel von der Heydte had little choice but to hide out in the local woods.

Von der Heydte and his men were to spend five days watching elements of three American divisions rumble up the very road they were supposed to have cut. The Jagdtigers never made it beyond the railhead in the northern reaches of the Eifel, thanks to American bombing. The only part of his ill-fated airborne operation that was successful involved dummies. Near the Elsenborn Ridge some 300 dummy

German paratroopers were dropped, causing some confusion behind American lines. Fearing it was a real air drop, American patrols were sent on a wild goose chase looking for German soldiers who never materialised.

While the Americans were thrown into a state of confusion, Field Marshal Montgomery was invigorated by the challenge of the German attack. Eisenhower's personal movements were hampered by suspicions that Skorzeny's American-dressed commandos were on their way to Paris to kill him. Monty sent out his liaison officers to report on what was happening on his southern flank. At Spa they found General Hodges' US 1st Army forward headquarters almost completely deserted, apart from two officers still in bed. Everyone else had retreated at short notice for fear of capture. Although Hodges was not under Monty's jurisdiction, he told his liaison officers to find him immediately and order him to block the Meuse bridges even if it meant using farm carts.

For ease of command, on 20 December Eisenhower reluctantly put Monty in temporary charge of all American troops north of the German breakthrough, which included the US 1st and 9th Armies. Understandably General Bradley was not happy with this arrangement, although it made sense. Monty meanwhile deployed 150 British tanks to the west of the river as a blocking force. He then asked Bradley's Major General 'Lightning Joe' Collins, commander of the US VII Corps, to put together a strategic reserve ready for a counterattack.

Men of the US 99th Infantry Division driving through Wirtzfeld. The 99th consisted of three infantry regiments, four field artillery battalions and a tank destroyer battalion. Their positions on the Elsenborn Ridge were directly in the way of the 12th SS Panzer Division.

Frozen-looking members of the 9th Infantry Regiment, US 2nd Infantry Division, taking cover from the German barrage in a snow-filled ditch at Heartbreak Crossroads in Krinkeler Woods.

Tiger IIs of the 501st Heavy SS-Panzer Battalion which formed part of Kampfgruppe Peiper. Although designed as a breakthrough tank, it was too heavy and cumbersome to be effective in the confines of the Ardennes.

An SS half-track rolls past a captured American vehicle as Kampfgruppe Peiper advances. This was one of a number of battle groups who spearheaded the 1st SS and 12th SS Panzer Divisions' thrust towards the Meuse south of Liège.

The Germans had 137 Panzer IV/70(V) tank destroyers available for the Ardennes offensive. The 1st SS only had ten, which formed part of Kampfgruppe Hansen. These vehicles were painted in the standard sand yellow factory finish that was then covered in circular patches of red brown.

Panzergrenadiers belonging to Kampfgruppe Hansen were responsible for destroying the US 14th Cavalry Group, part of Task Force Myers, on the road between Poteau and Recht.

(**Opposite, above**) Kampfgruppe Hansen panzergrenadiers running past burning American vehicles caught on the open road.

(**Opposite, below**) The Germans were reliant on mobile anti-aircraft guns such as this Flakpanzer IV Wirbelwind to keep Allied fighter-bombers at bay. The 1st SS Panzer Division had eight on its strength, which belonged to the 501st Heavy SS Panzer Battalion.

(**Above**) A Tiger II passing a column of American prisoners from the US 99th Infantry Division. They have a mixture of uniforms. Most have retained their helmets, but few have the luxury of a greatcoat to keep them warm.

(**Opposite, above**) This appears to be the same tank, seen from the rear. Two German despatch riders armed with submachine guns are keeping a wary eye on the prisoners.

(**Opposite, below**) Men of the 26th Infantry Regiment, US 1st Infantry Division, manoeuvring their 57mm anti-tank gun into position. Although the Ardennes region was largely defended by infantry divisions, most had their own dedicated tank, tank destroyer and field artillery battalions.

(**Above**) This grainy photo is from a German propaganda newsreel shot on 17 December and shows the crew of a Panzer IV belonging to the 1st SS passing more American prisoners. The young tank crew look dirty, tired and apprehensive.

(**Above & facing**) Men of the 12th Volksgrenadier Division, commanded by General Gerhard Engel, are seen here looting dead GIs at the crossroads in Honsfeld, Belgium, west of Losheimergraben at the northern end of the strategic Losheim Gap. The man in the foreground has had his boot stolen by the Germans.

Spent American artillery shell cases on the contested Elsenborn Ridge. The last German attack on 22 December 1944 was met by a deluge of 10,000 rounds.

Heavy American artillery such as this massive 240mm (9.5in) M1 howitzer was instrumental in breaking up the panzers' attacks.

Tanks of Lieutenant General Courtney Hodges' US 1st Army near Eupen. Colonel von der Heydte's ill-fated parachute mission took place just to the south.

# Chapter Three

# 5th Panzer Army Breaks Through

While Bradley, Hodges and Montgomery were trying to get a grip on the situation, Patton's divisions also found themselves under attack by panzers. To the south Manteufell's operations went much more smoothly than Dietrich's. For a start the going was much easier and the American divisions were weaker. In the centre General Walter Krüger's LVIII Panzer Corps, with two divisions, the 116th Panzer and 560th Volksgrenadier, was tasked with getting over the Our near Lutzkampen. It was then to secure Houffalize, and with the Ourthe river on its right it would move to cross the Meuse between Namur and Andenne. This certainly seemed achievable.

The 116th Panzer, known as the 'Greyhounds', had suffered during the battles in Normandy and the Hürtgen Forest. However, its ranks had been fleshed out with fairly good recruits and it had over one hundred panzers and assault guns. The 560th Volksgrenadier Division was formed from troops in occupation units in Norway and was poorly trained. Nonetheless it was to perform well.

South of Dasburg on Krüger's left was General Heinrich Freiherr von Lüttwitz's XLVII Panzer Corps with three divisions (2nd Panzer, Panzer Lehr and 26th Volksgrenadier). His orders were to get across the Our river, seize Clervaux and then hold the road junction at Bastogne. Lüttwitz was to cross the Meuse south of Namur.

The 2nd Panzer under Colonel Meinrad von Lauchert had been reorganised after Normandy and still had many veterans in its ranks. The division had over a hundred panzers and assault guns. Although virtually destroyed in Normandy, Panzer Lehr, under General Fritz Bayerlein, was rebuilding when it was committed to a counter-attack against Patton's US 3rd Army in the Saar region. As there was no time to draft in replacements before the Ardennes assault, the division was strengthened with anti-tank and assault gun battalions. The 26th Volksgrenadier Division, despite being an ad hoc formation, had a strength of over 17,000 men, so was able to offer welcome infantry support.

Another notable and quite powerful unit under von Lüttwitz's command was the armoured Führer Begleit Brigade under Colonel Otto Remer. This was formed around Hitler's headquarters guard and included a panzer battalion from the Großdeutschland Panzer Division, which was on the Eastern Front. To give it more punch the brigade had been reinforced with assault guns as well as 88mm and 105mm guns, in the shape of an artillery regiment and an anti-tank battalion. It also had its own flak regiment to help keep enemy fighter-bombers at bay. Infantry units comprised a panzergrenadier regiment as well as an additional grenadier battalion.

On Krüger's right units of General Walter Lucht's LXVI Infantry Corps were to cut off the Schnee Eifel salient prior to the capture of St Vith. Lucht's job was also to protect the junction of the 5th Panzer Army and the 6th SS Panzer Army. His command consisted of the 18th and 62nd Volksgrenadier Divisions. Both were of questionable combat value. The 18th Division had been formed in the summer in Denmark using men from a Luftwaffe field division and the Navy. However, it had garnered some two months of experience conducting defensive operations in the Eifel.

The 62nd Division only arrived in the Ardennes ten days before the offensive commenced. It included many Czech and Polish conscripts who spoke no German. The division was tasked with breaking through south of the Schnee Eifel and blocking the exits from St Vith to the south and west. Both divisions were backed by forty assault guns, but they had no tanks and little mobile artillery. Lucht's only armour was the 244th Assault Gun Brigade. For fire support he was mainly reliant on inaccurate rocket launchers.

Manteufell's line of advance meant that the brunt of his attack would fall on Cota's US 28th and Jones's 106th Infantry Divisions. The 106th was compromised from the start, especially once the 14th Cavalry Group had been forced to give ground. The division's three regiments were soon cut off from artillery support after the Germans got behind them. Although Monteufell's attacks were held at Winterspelt to the south and at Bleialf in the centre, to the north the American defences were pierced in the Losheim Gap. At his headquarters in St Vith Jones did not realise that he lay directly in the path of the northern wing of Colonel Hoffman-Schonborn's 18th Volks-grenadier Division.

In the meantime Manteuffel's XLVII and LVIII Panzer Corps were attacking Cota's 28th Division. He had deployed his three regiments along a north–south axis: the 112th was nearest Jones, with the 110th in the centre and then the 109th, which formed the boundary with the 9th Armored Division. The 112th managed to frustrate the 116th Panzer Division by stopping it from taking two bridges over the Our, while the 109th fought off three German infantry battalions.

Things did not go so well for Colonel Hurley Fuller's 110th Regiment. This had been deployed along an exposed supply route dubbed 'Skyline Drive' that ran parallel to the front. His men were manning isolated outposts. The XLVII Panzer Corps' infantry had soon infiltrated through the American lines, but before they could press on they had little option but to liquidate the American pockets of resistance in the villages of Holzthum, Marnach, Munshausen and Weiler. Nonetheless, just after nightfall Lüttwitz seized bridges across the Our at Gemund and Basburg, opening the way to Clervaux and Bastogne.

In the south Brandenberger's 7th Army moved to protect Manteuffel's flank. His LXXXV Corps threw the 5th Parachute Division towards Wiltz, and the 352nd Volks grenadier Division towards Diekirch. Further to the south the LXXV Corps' 276th Volksgrenadiers struck west of Echternach, supported by the 212th.

General Ludwig Heilmann's 5th Parachute Division was almost 16,000 strong and was supported by the 11th Assault Gun Brigade. Heilmann and his regimental commanders, however, lacked combat experience. At some 13,000 men strong, the 352nd Volksgrenadier Division was another of those infantry units that had been reconstructed using Luftwaffe and Navy replacements. Likewise the 276th Volks- grenadiers was made up of inexperienced and poorly trained recruits. By contrast the 212th Volksgrenadiers, with veteran officers and non-commissioned officers, was the 7th Army's best division.

The German attacks were held up by the US 109th Regiment, a Combat Command of the 9th Armored Division and the US 12th Regiment. By the end of 16 December German gains were quite modest, although they had breached both the Losheim Gap and Skyline Drive.

Frustratingly for Hitler, the American line had not collapsed wholesale and behind the scenes Eisenhower, the Supreme Commander, ordered the redeployment of the 7th Armored Division to the US 9th Army's sector and the 10th Armored, currently with Patton's 3rd Army in the south, to the Ardennes. Similarly Major General Matthew B. Ridgeway, commanding the XVIII Airborne Corps, was instructed to send his tough battle-hardened US 82nd and 101st Airborne Divisions to Bastogne. Clearly the German high command had miscalculated, for they believed the Allies had no reserves available, and yet within 24 hours Eisenhower had four divisions on the way to the battlefield.

German officers planning their attack route through the Ardennes. The poor roads in the region combined with the mud and snow would soon cause Hitler's forces major problems.

(**Opposite, above**) A German Sturmgeschütz III moving up for the attack. Note the American half-track to the left.

(**Opposite, below**) Knocked-out German half-tracks, which were used to transport panzergrenadiers. The second vehicle is armed with a short 75mm gun. An unidentifiable tank is just visible by the farm buildings to the left in the background.

(**Above**) American tank destroyers (such as this M10) employed by the tank destroyer battalions were more effective than the regular Sherman tanks, but were just as poorly armoured.

(**Above**) A concealed M10, serving with the US 1st Infantry Division, lurks behind a destroyed Panzer IV. This was among the positions of the 26th Infantry Regiment at Bütgenbach, to the northeast of Losheim and Honsfeld.

(**Opposite, above**) A Panther tank destroyed in the opening stages of the Ardennes offensive.

(**Opposite, below**) A tank destroyer of the 702nd Tank Destroyer Battalion, US 2nd Armored Division, on 16 December 1944.

A dead German fallschirmjäger. To the south the German 7th Army committed four divisions, including General Heilmann's 5th Parachute Division. Both its divisional and regimental commanders lacked combat experience.

Guns such as the US 203mm (8in) M1 howitzer were able to greatly disrupt German attacks.

The M4 Sherman proved woefully inadequate and there were too few of them until the arrival of reinforcements.

An M8 Greyhound armoured car leads a column through a devastated village.

(**Above**) A GI armed with the M1 Bazooka anti-tank weapon. Although an improved version was introduced in 1943, General Patton acknowledged that it was a weapon of last resort to prevent tanks overrunning infantry. In other words it was only good for defence at close range, rather than for tank-hunting. It proved invaluable in the woods, villages and towns of the Ardennes.

(**Opposite, above**) The Panzer IV/70 tank destroyer was deployed in large numbers for the first time in Hitler's Ardennes offensive. However, being very front heavy greatly reduced its manoeuvrability.

(**Opposite, below**) Once the heavy snow set in, fighting conditions in the Ardennes became really miserable.

# Chapter Four

# 1st SS Thrusts West

Although Obersturmbannführer Joachim Peiper's battlegroup from the 1st SS Panzer Division had got to Stavelot by the evening of 17 December, the rest of the division was lagging miles behind. It was held up east of Bullingen by unwelcome traffic jams, while the 3rd Parachute Division was 8 miles behind him. Likewise, the 12th SS Panzer Division was supposed to be on his right at Malmédy, but instead was bogged down by American resistance 14 miles to the east. The clock was ticking.

From a hill east of the Amblève river Peiper could see Stavelot full of American trucks. Defending the place was a single squad of the US 291st Engineer Battalion. To the south side of the river bridge this unit, equipped only with small arms, a bazooka and mines, set up a roadblock. They knocked out Peiper's lead panzer, forcing him to call a halt for the night. Although some American infantry reached the town during the darkness, Peiper breached their defences to the north the following day. His panzers were soon racing for the bridges at Trois Ponts to the southwest, which would put him on the road to Werbomont.

At Trois Ponts there were three river bridges to be taken, one over the Amblève and two over the Salm. The village was held by Major Robert Yates's Company C, 51st Engineers, who had arrived at midnight on 17 December. He had 140 men, with ten machine guns and eight bazookas. He ordered his men to prepare the Amblève bridge for demolition and sent a squad to the railway bridge just to the northeast. They were reinforced by a 57mm anti-tank gun separated from a company of the US 526th Armored Infantry who had been driven out of Stavelot.

Just before midday nineteen panzers coming up the road running north of the Amblève began firing on the men working on the river bridge. However, at the railway bridge the column was brought to a halt by the concealed American anti-tank gun. It took the Germans 15 minutes to find it and destroy it, along with its brave crew, but this bought the demolition teams enough time to destroy both the Amblève bridge and the northern one over the Salm.

Peiper was now forced northeastwards towards La Gleize and Stoumont. Some of his tanks headed for Werbomont but the skies had cleared of low cloud and they were pounced on by four Thunderbolts of the US 365th Fighter Group, which claimed two tanks and seven half-tracks. To make matters worse, ahead of him another squad from the US 291st Engineering Battalion had blown the bridge over the Lienne near Chevron. This stopped Peiper reaching Werbomont and halted his thrust on the Meuse.

Further north his men got over another bridge and swung southwestwards towards Werbomont only to run into an American ambush conducted by a unit from the US 30th Infantry Division. This was moving into position northwest of Peiper while the US 82nd Airborne was moving in from the west.

By late 18 December Peiper knew that the only way for his battlegroup to move westwards was through the village of Stoumont. Early that day the 117th Infantry from the US 30th Division reached Malmédy and Stavelot. The 1st Battalion recaptured Stavelot and cut the bridge over the Amblève. By the end of the day the 199th Infantry was at Stoumont, with the 3rd Battalion in the town, the 2nd Battalion blocking the westward road and the 1st Battalion acting as reserve on the high ground to the north.

Dietrich had been slowed down, and Peiper's spearhead had been blocked at Trois Ponts and Cheneux and he would have a tough fight on his hands if he tried to take Stoumont. He was cut off from ammunition and fuel supplies and the 3rd Parachute Division was stuck holding the northern flank of the advance. Even worse, the 12th SS was some 20 miles behind him, battling to get through the troublesome US 99th, 2nd and 1st Divisions on the Butgenbach–Malmédy road. The 2nd SS and 9th SS Panzer Divisions, which constituted Dietrich's second wave, were stuck back at the Siegfried Line thanks to the continuing traffic jams in front of them.

Early on 19 December Peiper threw his men at the American defences at Stoumont. His attack force included a mixed tank battalion with Panzer IV and Panthers from the 1st SS Panzer Regiment and a few Tigers, backed by a battalion of men from the 2nd SS Panzergrenadiers, an anti-aircraft gun unit, a battery of 105mm self-propelled guns and a company from the 3rd Parachute Division. Defending Stoumont was the US 3rd Battalion of the 119th Infantry supported by the guns of the 823rd Tank Destroyer Battalion. In the fierce close-quarter fighting that followed, two of the three American infantry companies were destroyed.

To the north the 1st Battalion had little choice but to withdraw, covered by ten tanks of the 743rd Tank Battalion, via Targnon to Stoumont. When the panzers ventured beyond Targnon they were shelled by the 197th Field Artillery and forced back. Now running out of fuel, Peiper gathered his battlegroup at Stoumont, La Gleize and Cheneux. He was running out of options. At this stage more American reinforcements arrived to help the 199th in the shape of ten tanks under Captain James Berry from the 740th Tank Battalion. This was very much an ad hoc unit made up of mechanics and repaired tanks from the US 1st Army's workshops.

The Americans now began to squeeze Peiper's forces. The US 82nd Airborne Division was pushing eastwards from Werbomont, and units were heading for La Gleize, Trois Ponts and Hotton. Advancing from the north was the US 3rd Armored Division with Combat Command B moving to help the 117th Infantry at Stavelot and the 119th at Stoumont. The rest of the division moved west of the 82nd Airborne to block the Germans driving from Houffalize and Bastogne.

On 20 December the Americans struck back, with the 1st Battalion of the 119th Infantry Division and the tanks of the 740th advancing through Targnon. Company C with five Shermans under Lieutenant Powers bumped into a Panther which they knocked out at close range. A Tiger tank proved a tougher foe but it was successfully dealt with by a 90mm self-propelled anti-tank gun. Powers then destroyed a second Panther by bouncing an anti-tank round off the road and up into the underside of the tank.

By nightfall Company C was on the outskirts of Stoumont, having occupied the local Saint Edouard sanatorium. However, that night the Germans counterattacked, driving the defenders out of Festung Sankt-Edouard except for eleven men under Sergeant William Widener who clung on in a small annex building.

When Task Force Jordan, from the 3rd Armored Division, tried to push southwards down the Spa road into Stoumont they were driven off by concealed Panthers. Nonetheless, Task Force Lovelady, also from the 3rd Armored, cut the road between La Gleize and Trois Ponts. They also intercepted and destroyed a supply column trying to get through to the beleaguered Peiper and his men.

While the US 504th Parachute Infantry of the 82nd Airborne fought to drive the 2nd SS Panzergrenadiers from Cheneux, all three battalions of the 119th Infantry struck towards Stoumont again from the north, west and east and succeeded in retaking the Sanatorium on 21 December. The following day bad weather brought the fighting to a halt and Peiper withdrew to La Gleize. He was refused permission to push eastwards to meet up with the 1st SS; instead he was left at La Gleize until 23 December. Permission was then finally granted and at 1am the following day he led 800 men through the woods along the Amblève, north of Trois Ponts and across the Salm river to reach his division on Christmas morning.

When the Americans entered La Gleize they found 300 German wounded, 28 abandoned panzers, 25 self-propelled guns and 70 half-tracks. They also rescued 170 American PoWs, most of whom had been captured in Stoumont. Remarkably, German resistance in the area lasted for two more days. Kampfgruppe Peiper had failed.

(**Opposite, above**) Members of the 1st SS Panzer Division in Honsfeld examining equipment abandoned by the US 30th Infantry Division.

(**Opposite, below**) This M10 tank destroyer from the US 30th Infantry Division claimed four panzers in Stavelot.

(**Above**) A German Panther and PaK40 anti-tank gun lost in Stavelot on the Amblève river. Although Kampfgruppe Peiper took the village on 17 December, the American US 30th Infantry recaptured it the following day.

The imposing bulk of a Tiger II carrying fallschirmjäger heading towards Ligneuville to the east of Stavelot. Tiger '222', commanded by SS-Sergeant Kurt Sova, was photographed at Tondorf, Deidenberg and Kaiserbarracke. It would end its days near the Stavelot bridge.

Seen here are men of the 1st SS reconnaissance battalion of Kampfgruppe Knittel at Kaiserbarracke.

A knocked-out Tiger II. Kampfgruppe Peiper had twenty of these tanks plus seventy Panzer IVs and Panthers. Peiper relegated its Tigers to a support role.

American M36 tank destroyers of the 703rd Tank Destroyer Battalion, attached to the 82nd Airborne Division, moving forward in heavy fog to stem the German spearhead near Werbomont, Belgium, 20 December 1944. This helped frustrate the advance of Kampfgruppe Peiper.

Two Panther tanks and a self-propelled gun lost south of Stavelot. Peiper was eventually forced to abandon all of his heavy equipment.

Two Tiger IIs were involved in the attack on Stoumont. Both were destroyed, with the second losing part of its gun barrel.

American soldiers of the 3rd Battalion, 119th Infantry Regiment, US 30th Infantry Division, taken prisoner by members of Kampfgruppe Peiper in Stoumont, Belgium, on 19 December 1944.

German-crewed Sherman tanks. Skorzeny's special 150th Panzer Brigade, masquerading as Americans, was supposed to capture at least two bridges over the Meuse at Amay, Huy or Adenne. Instead it became snarled up in the German traffic jams around Losheim and was forced to fight as a normal army unit at Malmédy.

A captured assault gun from Skorzeny's 150th Panzer Brigade, left abandoned and booby-trapped at Géromont.

This Panther, disguised as an American M10, was lost at La Falize.

Another of Skorzeny's counterfeit M10s.

(**Above**) This close-up shows how steel plates were employed to conceal the Panther's angular turret and make it look more like an M10.

(**Opposite, above**) This Wirbelwind was found outside the Saint-Edouard sanatorium at the western end of Stoumont. The Germans fortified the building but the Americans captured it on 20 December, only to be thrown out at midnight with the loss of thirty prisoners and five Shermans. A subsequent photo shows the flak guns blown up, with the blast causing more damage to the building.

(**Opposite, below**) These Wirbelwinds were used in a ground support role until they ran out of 20mm ammunition. They may also have run out of fuel as the one on the right has a Jerry can on its glacis.

(**Opposite, above**) Captured by the Americans, Tiger '204' was one of seven Tiger IIs lost by Peiper in and around La Gleize.

(**Opposite, below**) Another captured Tiger II '312' being used as a telegraph pole by signallers of the US 82nd Airborne Division.

(**Above**) After the 1st SS Division was driven back, it was discovered that it was responsible for the massacre of 362 American prisoners and 111 Belgian civilians in the Malmédy area.

(**Above**) The murders took place in a dozen locations, including Honsfeld, Büllingen, Ligneuville, La Gleize and Stoumont.

(**Opposite, above**) Belgian civilians killed in cold blood by the SS. Dietrich, Peiper and other senior SS officers would be put on trial for war crimes at the end of the war and found guilty.

(**Opposite, below**) A dead German soldier photographed on the streets of Stavelot in January 1945. A Sherman tank can just be seen in the background to the left.

Two shots of a Tiger II, lost in Stavelot, belonging to the 501st Heavy SS-Panzer Battalion. Peiper never had faith in the Tiger II contributing to his mission and he was proved right. It was wholly unsuited to the local roads and bridges.

# Chapter Five

# **Battle for St Vith**

The St Vith road junction west of the Schnee Eifel was the centre of communications in the northern Ardennes. Although the American defenders lacked tanks, they were reinforced by Combat Command B, from both the US 7th and 9th Armored Divisions. The 7th Armored had been first blooded in the fighting in September 1944 near Metz and saw action again in October in the Netherlands. In contrast the 9th Armored had yet to see action. German armoured units involved in the fighting included the 1st SS, 9th SS and 116th Panzer Divisions.

On 16 December St Vith was some 12 miles behind American lines and was acting as the headquarters for General Alan Jones's US 106th Infantry Division. The town was also host to disparate maintenance and supply units. Unfortunately for the defenders, the main routes west for Dietrich's 6th SS Panzer Army ran just to the north of the town, while those for von Manteuffel's 5th Panzer Army lay to the south. The problem for the Germans striking westwards was that they could not bypass the town as its continued occupation by the Americans would impede the flow of supplies and reinforcements.

Once the German LXVI Corps was attacking around Jones's northern and southern flanks, and the 1st SS had cut through the Losheim Gap, it was evident that St Vith was in danger of being cut off. Jones soon found his two forward regiments were trapped in the Schnee Eifel. Enemy units were in Setz just 4 miles to the east.

In Bastogne General Middleton with VIII Corps instructed Brigadier General Hoge's Combat Command B, from 9th Armored Division, to move on St Vith. General Gerow's V Corps also ordered Brigadier General Robert Hasbrouck's 7th Armored Division, held in reserve north of Aachen, to make for St Vith. His Combat Commands A and B were soon on their way.

Combat Command B of the 9th Armored found the going tough as the 14-mile route between Vieslam and St Vith was jammed with American forces all retreating westwards. It was not long before 9th Armored's Combat Command B, along with the 424th Infantry Regiment, was fighting to hold back the German 62nd Volksgrenadier Division near Steinebrück to the southeast, while the 89th Cavalry Squadron held Wallerode to the northeast. In the meantime the US 168th Engineer Regiment dug in on the edge of the pine forest just 2 miles from St Vith.

Brigadier General Brice Clarke's Combat Command B, of the 7th Armored, also suffered at the hands of US rear echelon vehicles clogging up the roads heading westwards. In the end divisional commander Hasbrouck had to resort to threatening to barge the vehicles out the way with his tanks if they did not clear the road. The rest of his division narrowly missed Peiper's panzers fighting south of Stavelot.

By nightfall on 17 December St Vith was protected by an American horseshoe-shaped defensive perimeter, which ran from Burg Reuland in the south to Recht in the northwest. The US 17th Tank Battalion was tasked to defend Recht, some 5 miles from St Vith. The village also acted as the headquarters of Combat Command R, 7th Armored. Remnants of the 14th Cavalry, which had been driven back by the German attack through the Losheim Gap, were in the area.

Defence of the St Vith–Schönberg road sector running northwest to Hünningen was the responsibility of the 87th Cavalry Squadron, 168th Engineers and Combat Command B, 7th Armored. The line to the south of St Vith was protected by Combat Command B, 9th Armored and the 424th Infantry, which was all that remained of the 106th Infantry Division.

Alarmingly, the Germans were now pressing to the west of St Vith. At Beho, 6 miles to the southwest, Combat Command A, 7th Armored was in action, as were the guns of the 16th Armored Field Artillery, which were shelling German units heading westwards. Colonel Austin Nelson's 112th Infantry Regiment, 28th Division, managed to reach the 424th Infantry and took up position on its right flank near Burg Reuland.

The German attack, though, was greatly hampered by all the chaos on the routes of advance. It was not until 2.00am on 18 December that the American northern flank at St Vith was tested when the 2nd SS Panzergrenadiers, supported by assault guns, forced Combat Command R, 7th Armored back to Poteau, 2 miles to the west. This unit was from the 1st SS Panzer Division and should have been supporting Peiper and his 1st SS Panzer Regiment battlegroup.

Shortly after the Americans were driven from Poteau, the survivors joined a scratch force known as Task Force Navaho and braced themselves for a third attack. Instead the German battlegroup moved northwards to try to reach the stranded Peiper at La Gleize. Over the next few days their attempts to get over the Amblève and Salm rivers were thwarted by units of the US 30th Infantry and 82nd Airborne Divisions.

In the meantime the Germans attempted to cut their way behind St Vith, just to the northwest at Hünningen. While the village was only weakly defended with anti-aircraft machine guns and two troops of cavalry, a counterattack led by Major Leonard Engemann with two companies of Shermans from the 14th Tank Battalion plus a company from the 811th Tank Destroyer Battalion gave the Germans a bloody nose. To the east of St Vith the fire of 275th Armored Artillery helped the 23rd and 38th Armored Infantry Battalions fend off two German attacks.

To the southeast the US 9th Armored and 424th Infantry were forced back by Colonel Friedrich Kittel's 62nd Volksgrenadier Division pushing up the road from the Siegfried Line. This placed the Germans within 3 miles of St Vith. Some 7 miles to the southwest at Gouvy the 116th Panzer Division was thrusting towards Houffalize, which lay northeast of Bastogne.

In the afternoon of 18 December Combat Command A, 7th Armored fought to retake Poteau. By nightfall the 48th Armored Infantry and 40th Tanks were in possession. However, the situation at St Vith did not look good. German armour was at Trois Ponts, 10 miles to the northwest, and had got past Gouvy 10 miles to the southwest. On the 19th the Germans probed the American perimeter.

Field Marshal Model and General von Manteuffel were fed up with the delay and descended on General Lucht, commander of LXVI Corps, and General Hoffman-Schönborn, commander of the 18th Volksgrenadier Division. Lucht was told in no uncertain terms to take St Vith as soon as possible. The 18th and 62nd Volksgrenadier Divisions were reinforced by Colonel Otto Remer's Führer Begleit Brigade. This consisted of a battalion of Panzer IVs, a battalion of assault guns, three panzergrenadier battalions, an artillery battalion and eight flak batteries. It had punched through the Schnee Eifel causing the surrender of the US 422nd and 423rd Infantry Regiments.

Once again traffic jams hampered Model and von Manteuffel's plans. Hoffman-Schönborn was only able to attack with the 295th Grenadier Regiment from Wallerode. American artillery fire beat this force off and Hoffman-Schönborn was badly wounded in the process. To the southeast the 190th Grenadiers of the 62nd Volksgrenadier Division ran into the US 27th Armored Infantry at Echelrath and its troops were mown down.

On 21 December Colonel Remer's men fought their way round the north of St Vith. The 105mm self-propelled guns of the US 275th Armored Field Artillery Battalion firing at point-blank range only just stopped them. The two Volksgrenadier divisions meanwhile began to slowly push in from the west and by nightfall they were in the town. With their forward companies overrun, the Americans had no choice but to set up a new defensive line, in the shape of a goose egg, to the west of St Vith. The Americans were helped by the poor roads. When the German columns rolled into the town there was once more an almighty traffic snarl-up. Model himself, hoping to view St Vith, had to get out of his staff car and walk in on foot. It was hardly the triumphant arrival he had hoped for.

By now the two Combat Command Bs from both the 7th and 9th Armored Divisions had lost half their Shermans and the surviving crews were exhausted. Likewise, the armoured infantry battalions had endured heavy losses, as had the

424th Infantry. General Hasbrouck at Vielsalm signalled General Matthew Ridgway, his new corps commander, suggesting they redeploy their defences beyond the Salm. By dark on 23 December all his men had got over the Vielsalm bridge and were west of the river, which was held by the 82nd Airborne Division.

On Christmas Day one hundred bombers from the US 9th Air Force pounded St Vith, flattening much of the town and causing huge clouds of dust and smoke to rise hundreds of feet into the air. Crucially, the Americans had held up General Lucht's Corps for a week and in doing so mauled the 18th and 62nd Volksgrenadier Divisions, as well as stopping the expansion of the gap formed by Peiper's lost battlegroup.

Men of the 504th Parachute Regiment, 82nd Airborne Division, supported by a tank. The division fought hard to hold the Germans in the Stavelot area.

Although Hitler's Ardennes offensive caught the Americans by surprise, they were not slow to react and swiftly sent reinforcements to St Vith and Bastogne. Trying to reach St Vith, the US 7th and 9th Armored Divisions found the roads clogged by units fleeing westwards in the path of the advancing Germans.

(**Above**) Sherman tanks rumbling through the snow.

(**Opposite, above**) GIs guarding a road-block with a 30 calibre Browning machine gun. Scattered positions like these struggled to hold back Hitler's panzer and Volksgrenadier divisions.

(**Opposite, below**) On 21 December M7 105mm self-propelled guns stopped the Führer Begleit Brigade north of St Vith. However, the Americans could not prevent the 18th Volksgrenadier Division capturing the town.

(**Opposite, above**) A Sherman shelling German positions. By 22 December the Germans had occupied St Vith, forcing the Americans to adopt a goose-egg defensive perimeter to the west.

(**Opposite, below**) An American 3-inch M5 anti-tank gun belonging to the US 7th Armored Division near Vielsalm, covering the American withdrawal from St Vith on 23 December.

(**Above**) Two members of this M10 crew find time for a quick cigarette and a smile for the camera.

The snow-covered ruins of St Vith. It was bombed on Christmas Day by the US 9th Air Force following the German occupation.

American crew cleaning a Sherman fitted with the 105mm howitzer. This was intended for a close-support role and was produced using the M4 and M4A3, as well as the horizontal volute spring suspension (HVSS) variants. This tank is undergoing maintenance: the exposed right-hand drive sprocket shows the track has been removed.

Shermans and other vehicles of the US 75th Infantry Division, which first went into action with 3rd Armored before the Ourthe river. The 75th Infantry included the 750th Tank Battalion, as well as two tank destroyer battalions.

A destroyed Panther. To the southwest of St Vith the battle was raging for Bastogne.

Youngsters of the
12th SS Panzer Division
captured by the Americans.
Such recruits showed Hitler
was running out of
manpower.

This photograph was taken on 29 December 1944, and the official caption reads: 'Sadzot, Belgium. Germans who died when the 509th Parachute Infantry Battalion of the 3rd Armored Division fought the 1st and 2nd Battalions of the 25th SS Panzergrenadier Regiment, 12th SS Panzergrenadier Division.' However, these men look more like fallschirmjäger.

## Chapter Six

# Battered Bastogne

While the battle for St Vith was under way, further south fighting was commencing for the other important road junction located at Bastogne. On 16 and 17 December the Germans had destroyed the US 28th Division's 110th Infantry Regiment and driven back its other two regiments to the north and south. General Middleton, the commander of VIII Corps in Bastogne, only had the Combat Command Reserve, 9th Armored and two engineer regiments with which to hold up the panzers. It looked as if Bastogne would fall quickly. Middleton, though, prepared to hold his ground.

By 18 December two American engineer battalions had taken up positions on the roads into Bastogne from the northeast, east and southeast. Early that day US Task Force Rose at Lallange came up against the 2nd Panzer Division's reconnaissance battalion. Shortly afterwards it was surrounded by Panzer IVs and Panthers of the 3rd Panzer Regiment and destroyed. That afternoon the Germans reached Allerborn and overwhelmed its defenders, and moved on to Longvilly. This was defended by a scratch force supported by four tank destroyers and 105mm howitzers.

To try to help out Colonel Roberts with Combat Command B, the 10th Armored Division sent three armoured infantry groups – designated Cherry, Desobry and O'Hara – to the east of Bastogne. In the evening Team Cherry, comprising Shermans of Company A, 3rd Tank Battalion, some light tanks, Company C of the 20th Armored Infantry, plus a reconnaissance platoon of the 90th Cavalry, took up positions on the high ground just to the west of Longvilly. That night the Germans captured the village of Mageret to the west of Longvilly, cutting the main road into Bastogne. At 11.40pm the defenders of Longvilly began to withdraw through Team Cherry, only to find the road blocked at Mageret, which the enemy had secured by 2.00am. Team commander Lieutenant Colonel Cherry, at his headquarters in the chateau at Neffe to the west of Mageret, was now unable to reach his men.

While the 2nd Panzer Division swung north of Bastogne, a screen of anti-tank guns was left to protect its flank from the Americans still in Longvilly. To the left of 2nd Panzer, General Bayerlein's Panzer Lehr Division had reached Niederwampach by 18 December. Here the poor roads and the horse-drawn transport of Major General Kokott's 26th Volksgrenadier Division held him up.

Although Bayerlein's battlegroup (comprising fifteen Panthers and a battalion of the 902nd Panzergrenadier Regiment) took Mageret, he was alarmed to learn that large numbers of Americans were still at Longvilly to the east of him. Bayerlein had no choice but to leave three panzers and some infantry as a blocking force behind him. Precious time was wasted. It was not until 5.30am that he continued westwards towards Neffe. Outside the village one of his Panthers hit a mine and the road had to be cleared; in the meantime his panzergrenadiers attacked Colonel Cherry's command post. Bayerlein's tanks had got to Neffe station by 7.00am, but inexplicably they stayed there for over an hour.

When the panzers finally rolled forwards again, they met Colonel Julian Ewell's US 501st Parachute Infantry Regiment, 101st Airborne Division. Ewell had been ordered to march east of Bastogne, locate the enemy and hold him. His forces successfully moved into Bizory, to the north of Neffe. The paratroops also reached Wardin to link up with Team O'Hara, but in the afternoon of 19 December seven Panzer IVs and elements of the 26th Volksgrenadier Division drove them back to Mont, southwest of Neffe.

Bayerlein and Kokott were troubled by the gathering organised resistance at Bizory, Neffe and Mont, as well as by the continued American presence at Longvilly. Instead of pressing on, Bayerlein decided to destroy the American convoy on the road between Mageret and Longvilly. At the same time Team Cherry tried to break through the enemy, in the process losing 175 men, 17 tanks and 17 half-tracks. Just a handful of men reached Bizory. At Neffe Chateau Colonel Cherry and his men held out until the evening, but with the building on fire Cherry had no choice but to withdraw the 501st Parachute Infantry to Bastogne.

To the north the reconnaissance battalion of the 2nd Panzer Division ran into men from Team Desobry at Bourcy at 5.30am on 19 December. After a 20-minute fire-fight the Germans withdrew and the Americans redeployed westwards to Noville, 5 miles north-east of Bastogne. There, under Major William Desobry, was the 20th Armored Infantry Battalion (though his Companies A and C were with Cherry and O'Hara), supported by a number of other units that included fifteen Shermans and a platoon of light tanks. Desobry had arrived at the village of Noville at 11.00pm on the 18th.

Looping north of Noville, 2nd Panzer cut the Houffalize road, knocking out two Shermans. At 8.30am two Tiger tanks loomed out of the fog but were met by a hail of American fire from a Sherman, bazookas and a 57mm anti-tank gun. Both tanks were knocked out but the Germans then began firing from the west. When the fog cleared at 10.30am, the Americans saw thirty panzers in the open ground between Bourcy and Noville; another fourteen could be seen to the south. Desobry, reinforced by a platoon of tank destroyers, managed to knock out nine enemy tanks and a shaken 2nd Panzer withdrew.

When Desobry requested permission to retreat to Foy he was reinforced by a battalion of paratroopers. Three companies of the latter counterattacked towards the high ground to the east and north of Noville, supported by Desobry's tanks. The Germans were waiting in anticipation of such a move. Only one American company reached its objective before being driven back to Noville.

Reinforced by tank destroyers of the 2nd Platoon, Company C, US 705th Tank Destroyer Battalion, the defenders ensured they inflicted a heavy toll on the approaching enemy armour. Unfortunately Desobry was severely wounded and Lieutenant Colonel James La Prade, the paratroop commander, was killed when an 88mm shell exploded nearby and shrapnel cut through their command post.

General Heinrich von Lüttwitz, commanding XLVII Panzer Corps, was frustrated at every turn. While the 2nd Panzer Division was stalled by the American defence at Noville, the Panzer Lehr and 26th Divisions had failed to get round or penetrate Bastogne's defences. In order to press on westwards only part of Panzer Lehr was available to help the 26th Volksgrenadier Division take Bastogne.

Early 20 December was again foggy and the Germans surprised the defenders of Noville. At 7.30am two Panzer IVs rumbled south down the Houffalize road and into the village. The Americans, though, were swift to react and a Sherman supported by bazooka fire knocked out both enemy tanks. What followed was a series of uncoordinated German tank and infantry attacks that were all beaten off. When the fog lifted, the defenders were presented with the spectacle of fifteen panzers and supporting infantry attacking from the south.

The American tank destroyers armed with 90mm guns killed four of the panzers, but a fifth – in the shape of a Tiger – advanced into the village. A Sherman tank crew, dicing with death because their turret had jammed, pumped three rounds into the Tiger. To their horror these rounds just bounced off, but the hapless Sherman was saved by the apparent inexperience of the Tiger's crew. The lumbering beast backed off and over a jeep which fouled a track, and this caused the Tiger to swing round, crashing into a half-track and toppling over onto its side. The crew fled on foot and the Americans destroyed the stricken Tiger with a grenade.

Major Robert Harwick, in charge at Noville, was now ordered to fight his way south to Foy. Just outside the village a traffic jam developed which was attacked by the Germans and confusion reigned as everyone sought to negotiate the road-blocks created by knocked-out Shermans. In the meantime the Germans were not only attacking Foy but also Mont, Neffe and Marvie, but everywhere they were driven off.

The ongoing fighting was bitter and often confused. At Marvie southeast of Bastogne the defenders were attacked by four panzers and six half-tracks carrying infantry. Team O'Hara's Shermans engaged the enemy tanks, destroying two and driving a third back into the woods to the southeast. The fourth got into the village but was knocked out by a bazooka team. The half-tracks also got into the village and there German troops fought men of the US 2nd Battalion, 327th Glider Infantry. The defenders lost 5 killed and 15 wounded, the Germans 30 dead and 20 captured.

By this stage the US 9th and 10th Armored Divisions had lost sixty tanks, Combat Command R of the 9th Armored had ceased to exist, and the 506th's 1st Battalion had lost half its men. The Germans, though, were now three days behind schedule and the Americans had successfully reinforced their defence of Bastogne. Many of the American stragglers, especially artillery units, were rounded up, turned about and committed to the defence.

On the evening of 20 December a battalion of the 77th Grenadier Regiment, 26th Volksgrenadiers, attempted to reach Bastogne from the northeast by forcing a gap between the US 501st and 506th Parachute Infantry, but the Germans were cut off and lost 235 men killed or captured. The temperature now fell and it began to snow heavily.

In Bastogne General Anthony McAuliffe, commander of the US 101st Airborne, was beginning to run out of artillery ammunition. By 22 December he was rationed to ten rounds per gun per day. His forward observers were instructed only to call on fire support if there was a serious threat. At noon that day four Germans, including two officers, arrived at the positions of Company F, 327th Glider Infantry, carrying a white flag and bearing a written message calling for the Americans to surrender. This was sent to McAuliffe, whose famous response was 'Aw, Nuts!' This was relayed back to the Germans with the explanation that 'Nuts' meant 'Go to Hell'. That afternoon McAuliffe received welcome word from VIII Corps that the 4th Armored Division was fighting its way north to relieve Bastogne.

The following day 241 Allied aircraft dropped 114 tons of supplies, followed by 160 aircraft with a further 100 tons the next day. The ammunition was welcome, but food for the garrison remained in critically short supply. On Christmas Day eleven gliders brought in a field surgical team and fuel. McAuliffe and his staff, with a decorated 2ft-tall fir tree on their table, looked a very sombre party during their Christmas dinner. Then on 26 December 289 aircraft delivered mainly artillery ammunition. German flak caused some losses and forced landings, but this show of American logistical muscle can have only dismayed the cold and hungry Germans. Between 23 December and 28 December Allied transport aircraft dropped nearly 1,000 tonnes of desperately needed supplies. The Germans managed to shoot down nineteen aircraft and badly damage another fifty.

Inside the Bastogne perimeter the supply staffs scoured local farms, shops and warehouses to boost their meagre food rations. After the 101st Airborne Division's field hospital had been captured on 19 December, the 501st Parachute Infantry's aid station in Bastogne became the main hospital. Wounded were evacuated to the west until the 21st, when the Germans cut the road. Two days later the skies began to clear and German columns were pinpointed by the tracks they left in the snow. Some

250 sorties a day were flown by US fighter-bombers in support of the garrison. 'The Battered Bastards of Bastogne', as the 101st styled themselves, were grateful that they had not been forgotten by the flyboys.

The Luftwaffe were not entirely inactive and bombed the town. The command post of the 10th Armored in the Hotel Lebrun was hit. The doll on their Christmas tree was damaged and in a moment of humour was awarded the Purple Heart. Kokott, despairing of ever taking the ruins of Bastogne, renewed his pressure. There followed a bitter battle for Marvie, with the Americans almost being driven out. American fighter-bombers harried the retiring German units, but also mistakenly bombed Marvie twice, much to the dismay of the American defenders. Kokott's control of the battle was now rapidly slipping away because on his southern flank the German 5th Parachute Division was giving ground to the US 4th Armored Division. This necessitated him despatching units to help the paratroops.

Kokott now switched to attacking Bastogne from the west with Champs, Flamizoulle and Hemroulle as his objectives. At Champs the American 502nd Parachute Infantry fought hand-to-hand with the German 77th Fusilier Regiment. Some eighteen German tanks rolled through the positions of the 3rd Battalion, 327th Glider Infantry, and divided into two groups, with one group heading for Hemroulle and the other north to Rolle. A single Panzer IV made it into Champs, where it was pounded into flames by a 57mm anti-tank gun and bazookas. At Hemroulle a lone Panzer IV got into the village and was captured intact.

Team Cherry, part of Combat Command B, 10th Armored Division Reserve, was moved out of Bastogne to reinforce the 502nd and 327th, but they and their supporting tank destroyers had already stabilised the situation. All of the German tanks and most of the two infantry battalions committed to the latest attacks had been destroyed, killed or captured.

The next day, 26 December, the US 4th Armored Division cut through the German 5th Parachute Division at Assenois, to the south of Bastogne. Lieutenant Colonel Creighton Abrams, in charge of the lead tank battalion, presented himself to General McAuliffe at 5.10pm. That night the first of forty supply lorries and seventy ambulances rolled into Bastogne. The battle was far from over but the German stranglehold on the town had been broken. Without Bastogne, Hitler's Ardennes offensive was now completely stalled.

(**Opposite, above**) Crews of Company B, 630th Tank Destroyer Battalion, US 28th Infantry Division, in their foxholes at Wiltz, east of Bastogne. They had lost their vehicles so had to fight as infantry.

(**Opposite, below**) Brigadier General Anthony McAuliffe with men of the US 101st Airborne Division. Known as the 'Screaming Eagles', these veterans of the jumps in Normandy and Holland were given the task of holding Bastogne at all costs.

(**Above**) Bazooka men from the US 28th Infantry Division pulling back from Wiltz. The three days of fighting there helped gain the 101st Airborne time to set up their defensive perimeter around Bastogne.

(**Above**) A bazooka team from the US 101st Airborne guarding one of the approach roads into Bastogne. The American bazooka proved an ideal weapon during the street fighting in the region's towns and villages.

(**Opposite, above**) A wary patrol keeping their heads down. Visibility was so poor that it was very easy to be on top of the enemy before realising what had happened.

(**Opposite, below**) GIs from the US 28th Infantry Division marching into Bastogne on 20 December 1944. They were regrouped into security platoons to help with the defence of the town.

A wrecked M18 Hellcat tank destroyer. The Hellcats of the US 705th Tank Destroyer Battalion supporting the 1st Battalion, 506th Parachute Infantry Regiment, helped to knock out thirty panzers.

Paratroopers of the 101st pass comrades killed during the Christmas Eve bombing of Bastogne.

Frozen-looking GIs queue for field rations. Keeping the troops fed and warm during the siege was no easy task.

General McAuliffe, fourth from the left, and his staff at a rather sombre Christmas dinner in Bastogne. However, they knew their ordeal was almost over as the US 4th Armored Division was coming to their rescue.

200483

(**Above**) American infantry taking aim at targets in the Bastogne area.

(**Opposite, above**) German troops killed trying to take the 101st Airborne's command post in Bastogne, 25 December 1944. Despite attacks by the 26th and 39th Volksgrenadier Divisions and elements of the Panzer Lehr Division and the 15th Panzergrenadier Division, the American perimeter never cracked.

(**Opposite, below**) GIs in snow camouflage shelter behind a whitewashed Sherman near Bastogne.

(**Opposite, above**) After the cloud cleared, American fighter-bombers were able to operate in support of Bastogne. From 23 December 1944 Republic P-47 Thunderbolts of the US 9th Air Force flew more than a thousand ground-attack missions delivering bombs and rockets.

(**Opposite, below**) German prisoners burying 101st Airborne casualties at Bastogne.

(**Above**) A much-needed supply drop. During the period 23–28 December 1944 almost a thousand tonnes of supplies was dropped to the garrison. This came at the cost of nineteen aircraft shot down and fifty damaged.

(**Opposite, above**) An M32B1 armoured recovery vehicle, a type based on the Sherman, belonging to the US 6th Armored Division, pictured in Bastogne on 14 January 1945.

(**Opposite, below**) A GI inspects an abandoned Panther. It appears to have a very basic two-tone camouflage pattern of sand and either olive green or brown.

(**Above**) A snow-covered Panther.

This flipped Panther was photographed in Houffalize to the north of Bastogne. It was a good tank, but the close-quarter combat in the confines of the forests and streets of the Ardennes neutralised many of its advantages.

## Chapter Seven

# Patton Strikes Back

The Battle of the Bulge was exactly the type of rough and ready scrap that General Patton relished. Just three days after the German offensive opened Eisenhower had ordered Patton and his US 3rd Army, comprising the III, VIII and XII Corps, to move north to attack the left flank of the German assault. But Patton was already ahead of the game, having ordered his III Corps to move from Metz to the north of Luxembourg. Its 4th Armored Division under Major General Hugh Gaffey moved to Longwy, while XII Corps' 80th Infantry Division was sent to Luxembourg. Both these tough divisions had most recently seen combat during Patton's push to the Saar river, and they were also veterans of Normandy. Gaffey's 4th Armored had seen heavy fighting in Lorraine and Major General McBride's 80th Infantry had fought hard to get over the Moselle river.

Patton's XII Corps under Major General Manton Eddy also included the 4th and 5th Infantry Divisions and the 10th Armored Division, minus Combat Command B in Bastogne, Combat Command A of 9th Armored, plus the 109th Infantry from the 28th Division. The plan was that Major General John Millikin's III Corps would relieve Bastogne. Millikin was told by Patton to 'attack in column of regiments and drive like hell'. The only snag was that some of the routes north and the bridges had been destroyed by the Americans to stop the Germans turning south.

General Barton's 4th Infantry was a highly experienced unit. His men were D-Day veterans, having landed on Utah beach. After fighting in Normandy, they helped liberate Paris, then penetrated the Siegfried Line on the Schnee Eifel and fought in the Hürtgen Forest. General Irwin's 5th Infantry had arrived in Normandy in July and had suffered heavy losses during the fighting for Metz. In contrast, General Morris's 10th Armored troops were largely greenhorns. Morris's division had not entered the line in Lorraine until late September, in time to take part in the encirclement of Metz and the drive to the Saar.

Patton's H-Hour was 6.00am on 22 December. The 80th Division moved on Merzig and came into contact with the German 352nd Volksgrenadier Division, which they cut through to reach Heiderscheid and Ettelbruck. This helped take pressure off the 4th Armored's thrust to Bastogne by holding up both the 352nd and 79th Volksgrenadier Divisions. On the left the US 26th Infantry Division took

Grosbous from the Germans but was checked at Arsdorf and Rambrouch by the Führer Grenadier Brigade, which consisted of a battalion of Panzer IVs and Panthers, a battalion of mechanised panzergrenadiers and a battalion of infantry. The 26th Infantry, commanded by General Willard Paul, had only just been pulled from the line to take in replacements after fighting near Verdun so was nowhere near combat-ready.

On the western flank III Corps was led by Combat Command A of the 4th Armored Division, which pushed up the Arlon–Bastogne road, with Combat Command B to the west using the secondary roads. At Martelange Combat Command A was held up by a German parachute company until 23 December, when the village was secured and the bridge over the Sûre repaired.

In contrast, Combat Command B reached Burnon by midday on 22 December, just 7 miles south of Bastogne. Here, though, the troops were delayed by more demolition damage and elements of the German 5th Parachute Division. The village was not secured until midnight and heavy resistance was encountered at Chaumont, which was also defended by Luftwaffe fighter aircraft. Some twenty-two Shermans of the 8th Tank Battalion and supporting infantry moved round the village and, despite a slight thaw that caused some of the tanks to bog down, captured Chaumont.

General Kokott was not complacent about this threat developing on his left flank and launched a counterattack with units from the 11th Assault Gun Brigade and the 39th Grenadier Regiment. This force emerged from the woods to the north of Chaumont and drove down the hill into the village before the Americans could react. Very swiftly sixty-five Americans were killed and eleven Shermans lost. By the end of the day Chaumont was once more in German hands.

That same day, 23 December, the US 35th Tank Battalion of the 4th Armored Division attacked the Germans holding Warnach to the north of Martelange. The village was held by a parachute battalion and a battery of assault guns, which successfully drove off the first attacks. The following day the Americans struck from three sides and once in Warnach fought from house to house. The defenders did not give up easily and counterattacked, claiming four Shermans and sixty-eight American lives. Once the village was secured, the Americans found 135 German dead and took a similar number of prisoners. When Bigonville was taken, the village yielded 328 German paratroop prisoners.

General Millikin's armoured thrust had been weakened by the efforts of the German 5th Parachute Division so he then decided to recuperate ready for another attack on Christmas Day. In Bastogne McAuliffe was understandably disappointed, but he remained optimistic that 4th Armored would punch its way through.

Tintange was taken after a costly struggle, along with Hollange and Chaumont. On the left Remoiville was pounded by four US artillery battalions. When the German defenders, who had been keeping their heads down, attempted to reach their firing positions they were mown down by American tanks using machine guns. By the time the fighting stopped, the Americans had captured 327 prisoners.

By 26 December the German 5th Parachute Division was in a precarious position. Its men were slowly being driven from their positions, killed or captured and its artillery was running out of ammunition. At nightfall the Americans reached Homprè, just 4,000 yards from Bastogne's defensive perimeter. Early on the 27th Lieutenant Walter Carr led a patrol in but it was not the first.

On Boxing Day the Combat Command Reserve fought its way through Remichampagne to the northwest of Chaumont and towards Clochimont. The plan was to hook to the left and through Sibret and then on to Bastogne. However, Sibret was defended by the German 26th Reconnaissance Battalion, so it was decided instead to carry straight on up the road through Assenios. This village was held by elements of both the exhausted 5th Parachute and 26th Volksgrenadier Divisions. Fierce fighting followed but the lead Shermans under Lieutenant Charles Boggess reached the US 326th Airborne Engineers at 4.50pm and 20 minutes later Lieutenant Colonel Abrams reported to General McAuliffe that the German siege had been lifted.

The tanks of Patton's US 3rd Army were given the job of cutting their way through to the besieged town of Bastogne, spearheaded by Major General John Millikin's III Corps and the 4th Armored Division.

(**Above**) Shermans moving up for an attack. The weather and the roads to the south of Bastogne greatly restricted Patton's line of advance.

(**Opposite, above**) Patton's 3rd Army crossing a river. His mantra was always 'Press on'.

(**Opposite, below**) An M18 Hellcat leading an American column. The combination of its 76mm gun and 60mph speed made it an effective tank-killer.

A knocked-out Panzer IV, a Panther and an American jeep caught in a US air strike supporting Patton's attack towards Bastogne.

Although Patton made good progress, German resistance still proved very fierce. This wrecked M10 belonged to the 654th Tank Destroyer Battalion, supporting the US 35th Infantry Division, which formed part of Major General Millikin's III Corps. From 22 to 25 December the 654th fought with the US 5th Infantry Division.

A Sherman tank of the US 4th Armored Division driving into the defensive perimeter of Bastogne. The ten-day siege was successfully broken on 26 December 1944.

By Christmas 1944 German losses were beginning to mount on their southern flank. In particular, the German 5th Parachute Division found it increasingly difficult to keep the Americans at bay.

(**Opposite, above**) The smashed remains of a German StuG III assault gun. This type of armoured fighting vehicle formed the backbone of the support for the German infantry units.

(**Opposite, below**) Men of the US 101st Airborne pulling out of Bastogne on 31 December 1944 after the siege was lifted. Their next task was to help clear the Germans from the surrounding district.

(**Above**) A member of the 101st Airborne killed during January 1945 during the operations to drive the Germans from the woods in the Bastogne area.

An American patrol in the Lellig area, Luxembourg, at the end of December 1944. Their snow camouflage looks to be makeshift.

A whitewashed M36 near Dudelange, Luxembourg, in early January 1945. This Gun Motor Carriage, based on the Sherman, was armed with a 90mm gun, enabling it to knock out both Panther and Tiger tanks at long range.

A group of American tankers examine their prize: a Tiger II captured during the Battle of the Bulge.

British Shermans moving up to take part in the Allied counterattack against the German Bulge. This involved General Horrocks' British XXX Corps.

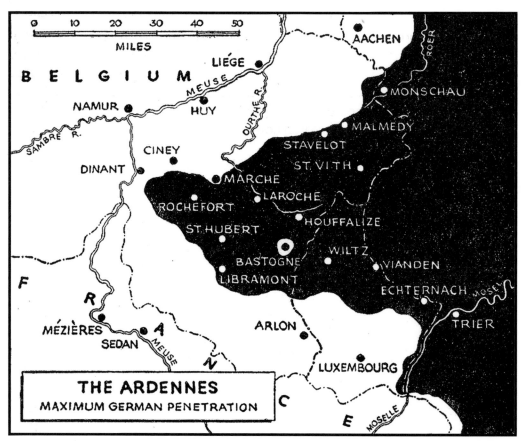

The panzers captured Rochefort on Christmas Eve 1944 and almost got to the Meuse at Dinant before they were driven back by an American and British counterattack. The Americans also counterattacked from the north and south and chose Houffalize as the point to cut off the German salient.

# Chapter Eight

# Drive on the Meuse

Hitler's assumption had been that in the face of the advancing panzers American units would flee or surrender. In some cases this did happen, but not in sufficient quantities to tilt the battle in favour of the Germans. Moreover, the German generals could have done without the distractions caused by American resistance at St Vith and Bastogne. Their goal was always the Meuse and beyond, but instead they became bogged down in the frustrating battles for the key road junctions. They had grossly underestimated how long this would take, and overlooked the constant need to keep feeding in troops.

While the fighting was still going on around Bastogne, Colonel Meinrad von Lauchert's 2nd Panzer Division was ordered to drive on the Meuse. His division had suffered heavy losses in Normandy and had been subsequently reorganised, but it still had numerous veterans in its regiments and was equipped with over a hundred tanks and assault guns. On 23 December the vanguard battalion of the 304th Panzergrenadier Regiment overwhelmed the US 4th Cavalry Group at Harsin and by nightfall was at Hargimont.

On 2nd Panzer's right the 116th Panzer Division found Houffalize undefended and its reconnaissance battalion reached Bertogne and Salle to the southwest, seeking a crossing over the Ourthe. American engineer and tank destroyer units thwarted this by blowing the bridges. This caused General Walter Krüger, commander of LVIII Corps, to instruct 116th Panzer to get over the Ourthe at Houffalize and strike northwestwards. This did the Americans a big favour as the original route was not well defended, whereas the panzers were now heading for the US 3rd Armored and 82nd Airborne Divisions.

By noon on 20 December both the 116th Panzer and 560th Volksgrenadier Divisions were north of the Ourthe and heading for Samrée and Rochefort. Both towns were defended by supply units of the US 7th Armored Division, which were swiftly driven out. In Samrée the Germans got their hands on 15,000 rations along with 25,000 gallons of fuel. This windfall was very welcome and enabled the 116th to refuel its vehicles. A counterattack by Task Force Tucker, from 3rd Armored's Combat Command A, was driven off with the loss of half a dozen Shermans. Two Shermans and a tank destroyer were also lost in the Samrée area.

In the Germans' path lay Hotton on the Ourthe, which was defended by 200 men from the 3rd Armored and a platoon from the 51st Engineers. They were supported by just one 37mm anti-tank gun, two medium tanks, two light tanks and two 40mm anti-aircraft guns. American reinforcements from Soy to the east helped beat off the attack although German armour got into Hotton, where the Americans knocked out three tanks, including a Panther. Resistance at Hotton convinced Krüger that he could not get to the Meuse via this route. He decided to withdraw to Roche, cross the Ourthe and move on Marche to the west.

On his right the 2nd SS Panzer Division was to strike for Manhay, which posed a threat to American defences stretched from Hotton eastwards to Trois Ponts. This 25-mile front was only thinly held by the 82nd Airborne and 3rd Armored Divisions. The key point was the junction between the two American divisions at the Baraque-de-Fraiture crossroads south of Manhay. On the morning of 21 December the American defenders drove off a patrol from the 560th Volksgrenadiers, and also captured an officer from the 2nd SS who was scouting a route for the panzers. The division was just 9 miles to the south waiting for fuel.

Not long afterwards men of the 4th Panzergrenadier Regiment, supported by some tanks, moved north of Baraque-de-Fraiture and cut the road to Manhay. In the process they captured four tank destroyers from the US 643rd Battalion, 3rd Armored, which were heading for the crossroads. On 23 December the Germans attacked Fraiture, just to the northeast, which was held by the US 325th Glider Infantry and were driven off.

In the meantime the Germans began shelling the crossroads. Then two panzer companies and two panzergrenadier battalions fell on the defenders. Although the defence of the crossroads was reinforced by three Shermans, Captain Junior Woodruff with Company F, 2nd Battalion, 325th Glider Infantry, requested permission to pull out at 5.00pm as their situation was precarious. Permission was denied and Woodruff's men were overrun. Just 44 of Company F's 116 men reached Fraiture.

The American position now looked critical as the 2nd SS threatened Manhay and the 116th Panzer was moving on Marche and Hotton. To the south 2nd Panzer was pressing for the Meuse. By the evening of 22 December Lauchert's 2nd Reconnaissance Battalion was just 4 miles from the river, having reached Celles east of Dinant. They were tantalisingly close to their first major objective. In reality, though, the Germans were horribly over-extended and had exposed their lines of communication. Obtaining sufficient fuel supplies was also a constant worry.

Certainly elsewhere things were not going so well for the Germans. To the southeast of 2nd Panzer, Bayerlein's Panzer Lehr Division had taken until Christmas Eve to secure Rochefort. On the northern shoulder of the German bulge the 12th SS Panzer Division had failed to break through the US V Corps. This stopped the

Germans from widening the breach created by the 1st SS. Only now were the 2nd SS and 9th SS Panzer Divisions able to get forward, but it was too late.

The danger for the Americans, though, was far from past. The German threat to the Meuse remained, as did the threat in the north with the commitment of the 2nd SS and 9th SS Panzer Divisions supported by the 560th Volksgrenadiers. In the north, controversially, Field Marshal Montgomery was given temporary command of the US 1st Army's V, VII and XVIII Corps. General Matthew Ridgway commanding the latter was not happy when Montgomery ordered the US 82nd Airborne to withdraw from their Vielsalm salient to a shorter line through Bra to Manhay.

The bitter battle for Manhay cost the Americans one hundred killed or wounded, along with nineteen tanks knocked out. Although the Germans were left in possession, they headed west instead of turning north into the rear areas of the US 1st Army. At Soy the 2nd SS Division was stopped by the US 75th Division. Ridgway instructed General Hasbrouck to retake Manhay, which he did on Boxing Day. At Marche and Hotton 116th Panzer was driven back, while at Celles the British Household Cavalry came up against the 2nd Panzer Division.

On Christmas Day General Harmon's US 2nd Armored Division, striking southwest from Ciney, split the 2nd Panzer Division in two in the Celles area. At Foy Notre Dame, just 4 miles from Dinant, elements of the US 2nd Armored and the British 3rd Royal Tank Regiment, 29th Armoured Brigade, attacked 2nd Panzer's reconnaissance battalion and some of its artillery units. They resisted until they were overrun, losing seven Panthers and 148 prisoners.

Further south, a panzergrenadier regiment, a panzer battalion and the rest of the artillery under Major Cochenhausen were caught in the woods between Celles and Conjoux. They were pounded by Allied artillery and fighter-bombers before 2nd Armored's tanks moved in for the kill. Cochenhausen and some 600 men fled on foot to the south and reached Rochefort, where the remains of 2nd Panzer had gathered.

Colonel von Lauchert was desperately short of fuel and had wanted to withdraw the lead elements of his division, but permission was refused. Attempts by Panzer Lehr to reach Celles were halted by Allied fighter-bombers. At Hargimont east of Rochefort Lauchert led a battlegroup almost as far as Celles but was confronted by massing British and American armour. His men came under artillery fire and air attack and pulled back to Rochefort. That day, 26 December, Hitler agreed to the withdrawal of 5th Panzer Army's spearhead and demanded the immediate capture of Bastogne. Although the fighting was not over, Boxing Day marked the end of Hitler's Ardennes offensive.

A formidable Panther tank rumbling through the forests of the Ardennes. Unable to swing north towards the Meuse river, by 22 December the 2nd Panzer Division had pushed westwards as far as Celles, just 4 miles from the crossing at Dinant.

Panzertruppen huddled round a fire next to their Panther. Although fighting in woodland was not ideal, the thick trees at least offered some protection from prowling Allied fighter-bombers. This crew must have been confident that the fire would not attract unwanted attention.

An M4A3E2 Sherman 'Jumbo' tank with the US 3rd Armored Division. This type of Sherman was up-armoured and just 254 were built. The presence of the 3rd Armored and the 82nd Airborne Divisions between Hotton and Trois Ponts prevented the Germans from swinging to the north.

A German Panzer IV and Panther destroyed during the close-quarter fighting in the streets of Hotton.

A German PaK40 75mm anti-tank gun with its crew dead beside it at Malempré to the east of Manhay. Why they were fighting from such an exposed position is not clear.

A 2nd Armored Sherman passing a knocked-out Panther. On 25 December 1944 2nd Armored split the 2nd Panzer Division in two in the Celles area.

(**Above**) American tankers warily examine a Panther – the Germans often booby-trapped their vehicles when forced to abandon them. This particular tank suffered a stoppage when a 75mm round jammed in the breech. Its crew had little option but to flee on foot.

(**Opposite, above**) A burnt-out Panther Ausf G. By the end of 26 December the two pockets held by the 2nd Panzer Division at Celles had been overwhelmed, with the survivors fleeing to Rochefort.

(**Opposite, below**) These Americans are examining the imposing bulk of a Tiger II dumped at the roadside. It may have simply run out of fuel; interestingly tow cables have been attached to the front of the tank.

(**Opposite, above**) A damaged Panther left outside the Hotel des Ardennes – the left-hand idler and tracks are missing, indicating it may have been under repair before the crew gave up trying to fix it.

(**Opposite, below**) This decapitated Tiger II was lost in the Ardennes. It also seems to have been under tow.

(**Above**) Another tank abandoned by the Hotel des Ardennes – this time a Sherman that had been pressed into German service.

American infantry marking
New Year's Eve.

A captured Ostwind flakpanzer.
The 1st SS Panzer Division had
eight of these with its panzer
regiment at the beginning of
December 1944.

A diminutive amphibious US M29 Weasel cargo carrier in Belgium, mid-January 1945. This vehicle was designed specifically to cope with such conditions and was used for resupply and casualty evacuation purposes.

# Chapter Nine

# **Defeat**

In the closing days of December 1944 the fighting around snow-covered Bastogne reached a climax. The 1st SS Panzer and the 167th Volksgrenadiers desperately attempted to sever the American lifeline into the town. To do so they had to cut their way through the US 26th and 35th Infantry Divisions. The latter had gained combat experience in Normandy and had fought to help stop Hitler's Mortain counterattack there, so they knew what to do. The German attacks were driven back by ground fire and air attacks that claimed fifty-five panzers.

Meanwhile the US 11th Armored and 87th Infantry Divisions to the southwest fought to widen the relief corridor. They ran headlong into Panzer Lehr and the 26th Volksgrenadiers, who had launched a counterattack. A fierce battle followed with heavy losses on both sides, but eventually the depleted German divisions were forced back to their start line. General Patton drove into Bastogne on 30 December to congratulate McAuliffe and his garrison.

The Battle of the Bulge, as it became known, was to have potentially serious repercussions for the British and the Americans. It was at this point that Montgomery completely overstepped the mark with Eisenhower. Unimpressed by the American handling of the battle, Montgomery renewed his call that he should be given operational control not only over his own 21st Army Group but also over the whole of Bradley's 12th Army Group. Monty's logic was that this chain of command would make it easier to liquidate the German bulge. As always, he was thinking of the military implications of such a move, and not the political ramifications. He did not appreciate that to take over at the very point when a major Allied counterattack was launched would be a slur on American military prowess. If Eisenhower agreed, it would be a vote of no confidence in General Bradley's handling of 12th Army Group. Behind the scenes it was common knowledge that, while his subordinates had shone, Bradley's leadership had been rather lacklustre.

Monty and the British press had already formed the opinion that he had saved the day. In the light of American bravery, tenacity and losses, this was an insult that could not be tolerated. Eisenhower, who had always shown the utmost patience and diplomacy with his British allies through some extremely trying times, decided that this was the final straw. He drafted a signal to the Combined Chiefs of Staff saying that either Monty must go or he would.

Fortunately for Monty, Major General Francis de Guingand, his very able 21st Army Group Chief of Staff, was aware of the mounting tensions and did all he could to defuse the dangerous situation. De Guingand went to see Eisenhower and informed him that Monty had no idea of the trouble he was causing, and asked for a stay of execution for 24 hours. He then flew back to Monty's headquarters and warned his boss that he faced the sack. At this stage of the war the last thing Monty wanted to do was lose his command. In addition, the situation would put Churchill in an impossible position because if he had to sack Monty it would cause an almighty political row in London.

There was no question of Eisenhower being replaced, which meant the war might be delayed while there was a tense stand-off between London and Washington. Fortunately Monty agreed to sign a message drafted by de Guingand promising full cooperation with Eisenhower and asking for his signal that had caused the offence to be destroyed. Eisenhower, ever the diplomat and content that Monty was contrite, let the whole incident pass. It was lucky that Eisenhower was not a vindictive man.

In the meantime the Allies completed their plans for a counterattack in the Ardennes. The intention was to cut the German salient in half at Houffalize, with Hodge's US 1st Army striking south and Patton's US 3rd Army attacking north. They would also swing eastwards towards Germany and the Siegfried Line. In order to free up the US 2nd Armored and 84th Infantry Divisions for the attack, General Horrocks' British XXX Corps moved to take up their positions west of the Ourthe. Supported by the British 6th Airborne Division, they were to deploy in the Marche area. The paras took over the foxholes of the frozen US 84th Infantry overlooking the German positions.

Horrocks was to move forwards towards Houffalize, to the right of the US VII Corps, with the 6th Airborne on his right and the 53rd Welsh Division to his left. Due to the transfer of the US 1st Army to Monty's command, and the criticism of the US conduct of the battle in the British press, there was some grumbling in American circles that Horrocks should be assigned a greater role. Monty, though, was right to hold him back, as 21st Army Group was short of reserves and to extend Horrocks' Corps further east would have been foolish.

Hitler was not finished yet, and he had up his sleeve one final grand but ultimately futile gesture as part of his Ardennes campaign. As the New Year commenced, the Luftwaffe belatedly sprang into action. Over a thousand German planes attacked British and American airfields, successfully destroying 150 aircraft and damaging another 111. Whilst this impressive massed attack came as a surprise, it was too little too late and it had minimum impact on the fighting on the ground. The Luftwaffe had to call on its air defence units, employing both experienced and inexperienced pilots.

In pressing home their raids, the Luftwaffe lost 280 aircraft and several hundred irreplaceable aircrew.

Undeterred, the Allied counterattacks commenced on 3 January 1945 amidst the snow, mud and fog. The weather once again greatly hindered Allied air support. In the following days frost and heavy snow made for firmer going, but hid German fixed positions and their minefields. In the face of very stiff resistance on the first day VII Corps managed to advance just 2 miles. The US 2nd Armored and 84th Infantry secured Beffe, and 3rd Armored reached Floret and Malempré. The British 53rd Division drove the enemy towards La Roche but came up against determined counterattacks by the 116th Panzer Division.

That day the British 6th Airborne fought all afternoon against Panzer Lehr to take Bures, suffering heavy losses in the process. Although the Germans held on to half the village, Sergeant Scott bravely drove in to pick up casualties. To his horror, a massive Jagdtiger rumbled round the corner and parked alongside him. When the commander emerged, he looked at Scott and the stretchers on his jeep and said gallantly, 'Take the wounded away this time, but don't come back. It's not safe.' The following day Panzer Lehr repeatedly counterattacked but proved unable to hold on to Bures.

By 7 January 1945 Horrocks' 53rd Division had captured Grimbiemont, just 4 miles from Marche. The following day his 51st Highland Division took over the attack and by 11 January was in La Roche. A few days later the British made contact with Patton's men. By mid-month Horrocks' forces were redeploying north back to 21st Army Group ready for the battles to clear the west bank of the Rhine from the Ruhr to the Netherlands.

Also by the end of the first week of January the US 84th Infantry had reached Marcouray and 2nd Armored had retaken Dochamps and Baraque-de-Fraiture. It was now that Hitler had to face up to the reality of his situation as there was little he could do to cling on to his hard-fought battlefield gains. Reluctantly, on 9 January he agreed to the withdrawal of 5th Panzer Army east of the Liege–Bastogne road. It was now that Patton commenced his main attack, employing the US 4th and 6th Armored, 26th, 35th, 87th and 90th Infantry, as well as the 17th and 101st Airborne Divisions. The going proved to be a tough struggle against increasingly desperate German units.

The 6th SS Panzer Army was ordered into reserve north of St Vith, though it would take it four days to comply due to Allied air attacks, blocked roads and the weather. German soldiers were not happy with what they saw as favouritism for the SS units, although few knew that they were actually destined for the Eastern Front so were hardly being done any favours by Hitler.

Stalin's winter offensive commenced on the Eastern Front on 12 January 1945 and two days later Hitler ordered the exhausted 6th SS Panzer Army east to defend not Prussia but rather Hungary's oilfields. Shortly afterwards, the US 1st and 3rd Armies linked up in the Ardennes. By 27 January 1945 American lines were back where they started when the Battle of the Bulge first commenced on 16 December 1944.

Hitler's grand plan had all been for nothing. Nevertheless, his Ardennes offensive proved to be a remarkable battle. Achieving complete surprise, he had thrown three armies at five US divisions over a 50-mile front. This resulted in an embarrassing breakthrough that brought the British and Americans to loggerheads. Manteuffel and Model, however, never came close to reaching Brussels or Antwerp. Despite some American units being thrown into a state of confusion, ad hoc battlegroups fought with bravery and distinction on the northern shoulder, at St Vith and Bastogne. This conduct greatly derailed the German timetable.

Hitler had severely underestimated the likely speed of the Allied response and the power of their air forces. Within the space of just four days the Allies had redeployed 500,000 men to the Ardennes. Once the weather had cleared, the German forces were at the mercy of Allied fighter-bombers. Their own airborne operations were ill-fated. The parachute drop during the attack ended in failure and the Luftwaffe's grand-slam came too late to influence the battle. Hitler also underestimated the terrain over which his armies had to fight. This slowed their advance and crucially delayed the second wave of attack forces.

The US armed forces paid a heavy price for their victory, suffering 8,497 killed, 46,170 wounded and 20,905 missing, captured or dead. German losses were hard to gauge, but it is believed they lost 13,000 dead and 50,000 captured. Other estimates have put German losses in excess of 90,000. The key point was that Hitler's armies, so carefully reconstituted and re-equipped after defeat in Normandy, had been thrown away. Some senior generals argued that they would have been much better used to defend the Rhine and Oder.

Stalin was to claim that his offensive saved the Allied armies. This, of course, was complete nonsense. Hitler's forces had already been fought to a standstill by then and the Americans had gone over to the offensive. Hitler had gambled and lost. He had thrown away the last of his armies and it was now only a matter of time before his house of cards came tumbling down around his ears.

(**Opposite, above**) A British Sherman Firefly in Namur on the banks of the Meuse. The British Army was instructed to help clear the German salient from the Ardennes by attacking eastwards towards Houffalize.

(**Opposite, below**) A British Sherman tank photographed in early 1945. At around this time the British media started reporting that Field Marshal Montgomery's 21st Army Group had 'rescued' the Americans – a claim that was wholly untrue and significantly soured Anglo-American relations.

(**Above**) Montgomery proposed taking charge of the American counterattack by assuming control of the whole of US 12th Army Group. Eisenhower was furious and wanted Monty sacked.

(**Opposite, above**) GIs from the US 75th Infantry Division rummaging in a Kubelwagen belonging to the 2nd SS Panzer Division at Beffe, south of Liege, on 7 January 1945.

(**Opposite, below**) German prisoners being rounded up on the southern front of the bulge. Patton's counterattack commenced on 9 January 1945.

The final resting place of Panther '413'.

Members of Company I, 3rd Battalion, 16th Infantry Regiment, US 1st Infantry Division, riding on a tank during their advance on the town of Schopen, Belgium, 21 January 1945.

When the snows melted, Allied intelligence units were able to take a better look at Skorzeny's ill-fated Panthers pretending to be American M10s.

Another lost panzer revealed by the thaw – in this case a turretless Tiger II.

British sightseers arrive in La Gleize to take a look at the abandoned Tiger IIs.

Time for a group photograph in La Gleize. The massive Tiger II broke down more often than not.

The glacis of a Sherman bearing a very crude German identification cross. Any Germans caught in American uniforms were shot.

The repaired bridge at Houffalize. Locals peer down at an upturned Panther that had been pushed out of the way.

Two Americans pose by an abandoned Panzer IV. In launching his Ardennes offensive Hitler squandered the last of his armoured forces. On the Western Front he was completely on the defensive from this point on.

# Further Reading

Beevor, Antony, *Ardennes 1944: Hitler's Last Gamble* (London: Viking, 2015).

Crookenden, Napier, *Battle of the Bulge 1944* (Hersham: Ian Allan, 1980).

Cross, Robin, *The Battle of the Bulge 1944: Hitler's Last Hope* (Staplehurst: Spellmount, 2002).

de Lee, Nigel, *Voices from the Battle of the Bulge* (Newton Abbot: David & Charles, 2004).

Katcher, Philip, *The US Army 1941–45* (London: Osprey, 1985).

MacDonald, Charles B., *The Battle of the Bulge* (London: Weidenfeld & Nicolson, 1984).

Neillands, Robin, *The Battle for the Rhine 1944* (London: Weidenfeld & Nicolson, 2005).

Pallud, Jean-Paul, *Ardennes 1944: Peiper and Skorzeny* (London: Osprey, 1987).

Pimlott, John, *Battle of the Bulge* (London: Bison, 1981).

Province, Charles M., *Patton's Third Army* (New York: Hippocrene, 1992).

Reynolds, Michael, *Monty and Patton: Two Paths to Glory* (Stroud: Spellmount, 2005).

Toland, John, *The Battle of the Bulge* (London: Frederick Muller, 1959).

Tucker-Jones, Anthony, *Armoured Warfare and the Waffen-SS 1944–1945* (Barnsley: Pen & Sword, 2017).

Tucker-Jones, Anthony, *Armoured Warfare in Northwest Europe 1944–1945* (Barnsley: Pen & Sword, 2013).

Whiting, Charles, *Ardennes: The Secret War* (London: Century, 1984).

Whiting, Charles, *'44: In Combat on the Western Front from Normandy to the Ardennes* (London: Century, 1984).

Whiting, Charles, *Massacre at Malmédy* (London: Leo Cooper, 1971).